A Newbie's Guide to OS X El Capitan:

Switching Seamlessly from Windows to Mac

Minute Help Guides

SOME PEOPLE ONLY HAVE A FEW MINUTES TO SPARE

Minute Help Press

www.minutehelp.com

Cover Image © f11photo - Fotolia.com

Table of Contents

Error! Not a valid heading level range.

Introduction: It Just Works

So you've decided to take the plunge and get started with OS X El Capitan for Mac. Congratulations! Longtime Mac users know that Mac just works — the interface you'll come to know and love is intuitive, powerful, and designed to make your life easier. Technology can and should be exciting, and your Mac will offer all of that excitement, without the headaches!

Whether you're a first time Mac user or a seasoned Mac devotee, OS X El Capitan has something for everyone. The El Capitan update brings Mac OS X even closer to the look and feel of iOS (the operating system for Apple mobile devices like the iPhone and the iPad). New features like Split View make it easier than ever to get things done, and design improvements make things look better than ever. Just like its cousin iOS 9, El Capitan features dramatic improvements to its Spotlight Search interface that make it more intuitive than ever to get the information you need. Mail will automatically pull in contacts and calendar events for you, so you never have to worry about missing an important phone call or meeting, not to mention the new Mail message full screen experience. There are also big improvements to established apps like Notes and Photos that help you organize and enjoy your photos, notes, to-do lists and more. Under the hood, El Capitan includes several tweaks that significantly improve your Mac's performance. Apps open faster, Mail messages load more quickly, and graphics are handled more fluidly. Just like the previous OS X upgrade (Yosemite), El Capitan is a free download through the Apple App Store, though if you're lucky enough to own a brand new Apple iMac or MacBook, it will ship with El Capitan pre-installed.

But wait, you say. You've never used a Mac before, and you have no idea what any of this means. No worries! This guide was written just for you. We'll cover everything you need to know about making the switch from Windows to Mac, the basic terminology you'll need to find your way around and customize your machine, some handy tips and tricks that even serious Mac users may not know, and some basic maintenance that will keep your Mac happy and healthy for years to come. Finally, we'll cover a number of free third party apps that will help you get the most out of your Mac and OS X El Capitan. Along the way, we'll give you lots of screenshots, tips and practice so that you can feel confident, competent and comfortable with your new Mac.

Congratulations on choosing OS X El Capitan for Mac — now let's get started!

How to Use This Guide

This guide will introduce you to your Mac and to many of OS X El Capitan's new features. If you're brand new to OS X, you may want to read through **Part 1: Making the Switch** in order to get your bearings. Then, try working through **Part 2: The Basics.** Try to keep your Mac on as you read so that you can try out features and tasks as you read about them. The key is to engage your muscle and visual memory as you read. This will help you remember things a little more clearly and help you connect your Mac's functions and features to the things you need or want to do with your machine. Don't be afraid to experiment, either! The more you explore your Mac, the more comfortable you'll feel.

After you've made it through Parts 1 and 2, look over **Part 4: Maintaining Your Mac,** to get a sense of how to keep your Mac healthy and happy.

Part 3: Getting the Most Out of Mac and **Part 5: The Power of Free** may serve you better as reference sections rather than chapters you read straight through from start to finish. There's a lot of information here, so be careful not to overload yourself. These sections have plenty of information for seasoned Mac users as well.

If you do start feeling overwhelmed, take a break! Rome wasn't built in a day, and you shouldn't push yourself to learn everything Mac in one day either. We promise, though, it'll come fairly quickly. Have fun with the process – Mac is easy to use, and we know you'll enjoy it!

Part I: Making the Switch from Windows to Mac

You are no doubt aware of the passionate nature of the Mac versus Windows debate. However, the two operating systems are much less at odds with each other than their respective devotees can seem to be, so don't worry! While it's true that OS X El Capitan looks quite a bit different from Windows, rest assured that you'll be able to accomplish just about everything you could do in Windows on your Mac and then some.

This section will outline the major differences between the Windows and OS X operating systems, give you a crash course in "Mac speak," help you find your way around a Mac keyboard, and give you some tips for migrating your files from a Windows system to a Mac running OS X El Capitan.

NOTE: *This guide is based on OS X El Capitan, the newest version of OS X. However, some of this information applies to older versions of the software like Mavericks and Yosemite. If you're running older versions of OS X, though, we strongly recommend installing El Capitan, available for free in the App Store.*

1.1 Introducing Mac OS X

Windows and Mac OS X are two types of operating systems. Operating systems are major pieces of software that control just about every aspect of a computer user's experience. OS X El Capitan is the latest version of Mac OS X. The operating system OS X has been around since 2001, and we've already seen Cheetah, Puma, Jaguar, Panther, Tiger, Leopard, Snow Leopard, Lion, Mountain Lion, Mavericks and Yosemite. With each upgrade, Mac has become more powerful, user-friendly, and easier for former Windows users to come to terms with. In OS X 10.9, Apple broke with its big cat naming tradition, switching to a naming convention based on California landmarks, which brings us to OS X 10.11, better known as El Capitan.

Vertical Integration

For the average end user, the main difference between Mac and Windows is the user interface – what you see and how you interact with your machine. We'll be covering this in lots of detail throughout this guide. However, another important difference between the two is more fundamental than looks alone. Mac OS X is designed to run on Apple computers – and only Apple computers, legally speaking. Windows, meanwhile, can be run on several different brands of computers – Dell, Toshiba, HP, etc. You can even run Windows on a Mac if you just can't bear to give it up! Apple's long-term strategy of connecting its hardware and software into one complete computing solution is called vertical integration.

While it can be argued that Windows is more flexible due to the fact that it's hardware-agnostic, Mac users benefit immensely from Apple's vertical integration. Your Mac's hardware and software are optimized for each other, resulting in better performance and less startup third party "junk" that frequently comes preinstalled on machines running Windows. Mac's famous intuitiveness also has roots in its seamless software and hardware design. In fact, this is the main reason why Apple runs two different operating systems – OS X, which is run on Apple computers and laptops, and iOS, which runs on iPhones, iPads and iPods. iOS handles hardware features unique to mobile devices, while El Capitan is custom-built for powerful iMacs and MacBooks.

Apple's long history of vertical integration also put it in an enviable position when mobile computing took the world by storm in the late 2000s. In fact, OS X El Capitan introduces some of the most powerful integration throughout the Apple iOS device family (iPhone, iPad, iPod, etc.) that we've seen since the first iPhone hit the market in 2007. If you use other Apple devices, OS X El Capitan will seamlessly unite your content and workflow across all of your Apple devices, with practically no work required on your part.

A Note About Compatibility

Programs, or, in Mac-speak, applications (apps for short) are smaller pieces of software that rely on your operating system to run correctly. This means that a Windows version of Microsoft Office won't work on a Mac computer – instead, you'll need Microsoft Office for Mac. Don't panic, though, if you're not ready to spend your hard-earned money repurchasing major software like MS Office – we'll discuss some free alternatives in **Part 5: The Power of Free**.

Long story short, when you install new programs, you'll be looking for Mac-compatible ones. In the past, this could be quite limiting, but due to Mac's surge in popularity over recent decades, most programs are now available in Mac versions. The App Store that comes pre-installed in El Capitan OS X is a great place to start looking for new apps, but you can also download Mac apps from elsewhere on the web if you need to.

File Formats

Your Mac is going to handle most of your Windows files without any drama. There are, of course, exceptions. WMV (Windows Media Video) and WMA (Windows Media Audio) files will play on your Mac, but you may need to do some tinkering if you want to manage them using iTunes.

For the most part, though, El Capitan will make file migration a breeze. The Migration Assistant Tool can be run during setup or later on, and we'll show you how in **Part 2.1**.

Now that you've got a basic understanding of the big-picture differences between OS X El Capitan and Windows, let's get a little more specific, starting with some terminology.

1.2 A Computer Task By Any Other Name...

Mac and Windows look quite different, but underneath the new look and feel, you'll find that the tasks you need to perform are fairly similar. You will need to master some new vocabulary, though.

The following table is a rundown of some frequently used Mac/Windows terms. Feel free to refer back to this table as often as you need to!

Windows	Mac
Windows Explorer / My Computer / Computer	Finder
Control Panel	System Preferences
Programs	Applications (often shortened to apps)
Task Bar and Start Menu	Dock
Tray	Menulets
Recycle Bin	Trash
Task Manager	Activity Monitor

1.3 Keyboard, Trackpad and Magic Mouse

Ok, enough theory! Now let's get into some mechanical differences between Windows and Mac that will affect the way you interact with your computer – specifically, differences between Windows and Mac keyboards and trackpads / mice.

Keyboard

Apple Key

Obviously, there's no Windows key on a Mac keyboard – instead, you've got an Apple key (⌘), which doubles as the command key. You'll find it just to the left of your spacebar. For keyboard shortcuts, it works just like the control key on a Windows keyboard - ⌘+c (copy), ⌘+v, (paste), for example. You may hear it referred to as the "pretzel key" or the "clover key", though older Mac keyboards used an actual Apple image instead of the current twisty symbol.

Control Key

The Mac control key is there for right click functionality. Ignore what you may have heard – you can and should "right click" on a Mac. One way to do this is to hold down the control key and click. Try it and see how it works!

Delete (Backspace)

On a Windows keyboard, the backspace button is a 'backwards delete' key (removing the space immediately preceding the cursor) and the delete button is a 'forwards delete' key (removing the space immediately after the cursor). On a Mac keyboard, the backspace key is labeled 'Delete' and is in exactly the same location as the Windows backspace key. The Windows delete key (forward delete) is labeled 'Del ->.' On smaller MacBook keyboards, this key does not exist. You can still forward delete by using the FN + Delete if you must.

Function Buttons

On a Mac, it's easy to tell what each function button does by the tiny picture assigned to the button. On newer Mac keyboards, F1 dims, F2 brightens, F3 opens Mission Control, F4 opens Launchpad, F5 dims backlit keyboards, F6 brightens backlit keyboards, F7 skips back a track, F8 pauses/plays media, F9 skips forward a track, F10 mutes, F11 decreases volume, and F12 increases volume. Go ahead and play with these function buttons. You won't hurt anything, we promise!

Magic Mouse / Trackpad

Traditional PC-based mice allow users to move the cursor/pointer around the screen, click, drag and drop, and maybe scroll. In El Capitan, you can also "shake" the cursor/pointer by wiggling your finger or your mouse to see an enlarged cursor icon. This is incredibly useful when you lose your mouse in a forest of app windows!

If you're using a magic mouse, you'll find one seamless top surface in place of the standard right and left buttons. While you will still use the mouse to move the cursor and pointer around within documents and apps, you can also use the entire surface of the mouse as if it were a trackpad. This allows Mac users to take advantage of multitouch gestures (see **2.3** for more).

And by the way, if you're feeling a little overwhelmed with all of this information, don't panic – it will all become second nature to you with a little practice. With that in mind, let's get started using your Mac!

Part 2: The Basics

Ready to get started using your Mac? This section will give you what you need to get up and running. So go ahead and fire it up by pressing the power button!

2.1 Setup Assistant

The first time you start a new Mac, you'll need to do some setup. OS X El Capitan makes this incredibly easy, but here's the order of operations.

1. First, you'll need to **select your country** (if you don't see yours, choose "See All").

2. Next, you'll choose your **keyboard layout** – if you're an English speaker in the United States, you'll probably be most comfortable with the U.S. keyboard, but if you're, say, working on a doctorate in Chinese literature, there are options for you, too. In fact, the El Capitan upgrade includes lots of international language improvements, particularly for speakers and typists of Chinese, Japanese, Korean, Hindi, Bengali, Arabic and Hebrew.

3. After you click continue, you can **choose a wireless network**.

4. If you do select a wireless network, it will trigger **Migration Assistant**. Migration Assistant will help you transfer files from an older Mac, a backup disk, or a Windows PC. Migration Assistant will automatically move files into their appropriate locations – music files to the Music folder, for example.

5. Next, decide whether or not to enable Location Services. Location Services allow apps to view your Mac's physical location. Many apps require Location Services to function, like Find My Mac, and many more become much more useful with Location Services enabled, like Maps. We do recommend enabling them, but if you have privacy concerns, you can certainly opt out.

6. The next screen prompts you to enter an **Apple ID**. If you don't already have an Apple ID, you can create one from this screen. It's a good idea to go ahead and set this up – it's free and will allow you to take advantage of the App Store and iTunes. Plus, it will allow you to set up iCloud - a must for Apple mobile device users! You can also use your Apple ID as your Mac login credentials if you wish.

7. If you've set up an Apple ID, the next part of the setup process is **Find My Mac**, powered by iCloud. Find My Mac is exactly what it sounds like. If your Mac goes missing, Find My Mac will allow you to pinpoint its physical location, send messages to it, wipe its contents, and lock it. Hopefully you will never need this feature, but if you do, you'll be glad you enabled it.

8. Almost there! Read **the terms of service** and click **Agree**.

9. And finally, here we are at your **account creation** screen! In OS X El Capitan, you can use your Apple ID and password as your account if you like, meaning you have fewer accounts to keep track of. If you prefer the traditional account creation method, though, you can enter your full name, account name, and password. The first account you create on your Mac is an administrative account by default. Be sure to pick an account name you can live with, because this will be very difficult to change in the future.

10. Now **select your time zone**.

11. Decide whether or not to send Diagnostics and Usage Data to Apple.

12. Click **Start Using Your Mac** – this is where the fun really starts!

2.2 Meet Your Mac

So here you are, staring at the vast expanse of your empty desktop. If you're a former Windows user, you may feel a little disoriented by all that wide-open screen space. So let's take a tour – it's nowhere near as barren as it appears!

You should be seeing something like this:

Menu Bar

At the top left, you'll see the menu bar. This is the only menu bar on your Mac, and the contents of the bar will change based on what application you are running. Right now, it's displaying the Finder menu (remember that Finder is the Mac equivalent of Windows Explorer). You'll see Finder, File, Edit, View, Go, Window and Help as available menu items.

Menulets

At the top right, you'll see several "menulets," which include Bluetooth, wireless connectivity, volume, battery, time and date, the name of the account currently logged in, Spotlight search, and Notifications, as well as other assorted third party icons.

Go ahead and click through your menulets – you won't hurt or change anything by clicking them, and it's good to know what each one does. Pay special attention to the magnifying glass (Spotlight) and Notification Center (the last menulet on the right). You'll probably be using these two quite often once you're off the ground with your new Mac.

Dock

At the bottom of the screen, you'll see the Dock, a strip of icons that provide quick access to frequently used applications. It's easy to customize, so once you've got a sense of the apps you use the most often, you'll be able to design a tailor-made dock just for you.

Use your trackpad or magic mouse to hover over each of the pictures in the Dock to see which applications the pictures represent. You'll see, from left to right, Finder, Launchpad, Safari, Mail, Contacts, Calendar, Reminders, Notes, Maps, Photos, Messages, FaceTime, iTunes, iBooks, App Store and System Preferences. We'll talk about them all soon!

If you've used a Mac running Mavericks or older, you'll probably notice that El Capitan looks a bit different. The cleaner, flatter design of the Dock and its icons brings it in line with the look and feel of iOS (and that of modern design). We were also thrilled to see that the "spotlight" that appeared beneath running apps has been replaced with a much easier to see black dot. El Capitan also includes a new system font called San Francisco, which is found on iOS devices and on Apple Watch.

To start an app from the dock, simply click on the icon. If you click on an icon while the application is open, doing so will bring the application window to the front of your screen. You may notice a light gray line on your dock. This is the "dividing line." To the left of this line are apps and to the right are folders, files, documents and the Trash icon. OS X El Capitan's Dock also includes a download manager. Clicking on this will cause a list of recently downloaded files to pop up.

Trash

At the right end of all the applications on your Dock is the Trash. To delete a folder, file or application, drag the item to the Trash, or right click the item and select **Move to Trash** from the pop-up menu. If you want to eject a disk or drive (such as an iPod or USB flash drive), drag the volume into the Trash. As the volume hovers over the trash, the icon morphs from a trash can to a large eject button. Release the mouse, and your volume will be safely ejected and can be removed from the computer. To empty the trash, right click (**2.3**) on the Trash icon in the Dock, and select **Empty Trash.**

2.3 Swipe-aerobics: Multitouch Gestures on the Trackpad/Magic Mouse

Before we go any further, you're going to need to know how to interact with OS X El Capitan beyond the standard point-and-click needed in a Windows world. So, limber up your wrists, because we're going to do some multitouch gesture swipe-aerobics!

Chances are you already know one "gesture" – clicking. Your Mac will happily respond to single and double clicking, just like your PC. Now, let's add something new to your repertoire – the tap.

Tap

Tap once somewhere on your desktop, using either the surface of your magic mouse or your trackpad, depending on your Mac. This is a tap, and it's the same as a click.

Double Tap

Now, tap with two fingers at the same time. Did a menu just pop up? That's because you just "right clicked" on your desktop! Remember, you can also "right click" using CONTROL + click – feel free to use whichever option works best for you.

Scroll

To scroll, move up and down in documents or side to side with two fingers (two-finger swipe). Doing so also activates the scroll bar which otherwise remains hidden in apps like Safari and Finder. Scrolling all the way to the top or bottom creates a 'rubber band' effect, where the page bounces down or up depending on whether you have reached the top or bottom of the page. You may already be familiar with this effect from iOS devices and apps, such as Safari on the iPhone or iPad.

*TIP: OS X El Capitan defaults to "natural scrolling," in which content follows the direction of your fingers. This is a personal preference, and if it's too disorienting, you can revert to normal scrolling. If you decide to turn off natural scrolling, check out Trackpad Options in **3.3**.*

Swipe

Swiping should be very familiar for anyone who's used an e-reader or an iPad or iPhone. To swipe, drag your finger on the trackpad or magic mouse. Notice that the mouse moves with your finger. In fact, swiping is just like using a mouse, but skips the middleman.

In OS X El Capitan, we need to practice two additional types of swipes.

First, take three fingers, put them on your trackpad or magic mouse surface, and drag them to your right. This should appear to move your whole desktop out of the way and drag in your Dashboard area (we'll explore widgets and the Dashboard in **3.2**). Later, you'll be using the three-finger swipe across to navigate between full screen apps as well. Note that if nothing happens, you may need to enable the Dashboard, which we'll explain further in **3.2**.

Now, take three fingers and swipe **up.** This triggers Mission Control. It lets you see everything that you have running. Right now, that's probably not much, but once you've got six or seven applications going, it can be a productivity lifesaver! Take three fingers and swipe back down to return to your desktop.

In short, "swiping" just means dragging your fingers either across or up and down the track pad. In OS X El Capitan, you'll want to be comfortable with two- and three-finger swipes as well.

Pinch

In some applications, you can "pinch" to zoom in and out. Take your thumb and forefinger and move them toward each other in a pinching motion. This will zoom in on pictures and web pages. The reverse motion will zoom out. You can also pinch to reveal all of your Safari tabs (**2.6**).

Five Finger Pinch

Pull all five fingers together to reveal Launchpad – a list of all the apps on your Mac that looks suspiciously like iOS. Move all five fingers apart from each other to dismiss it. We'll talk more about Launchpad in **2.6.**

Rotate

Rotate images using your thumb and first finger and twisting your wrist in the direction you'd like to rotate.

Got all that? Don't worry if any of these motions feels awkward at first – it'll be second nature within a handful of sessions on your Mac, we promise!

2.4 Tutorial: Getting to Know Your Mac with Photo Booth

All right, now we're ready to delve a little deeper into your Mac by actually opening and managing an application! We're going to use Photo Booth as an example to learn how to run applications in OS X El Capitan, so follow along on your Mac to start getting comfortable with Mac basics.

Find Photo Booth by typing "Photo Booth" into Spotlight search (he magnifying glass in the top right corner). Click the top hit to open the application. Notice how the Photo Booth icon starts bouncing in the Dock? That means that the program is opening. Once it stops bouncing, you'll see a small black dot under the icon, indicating that the app is running.

Running an Application

Now you should be staring at yourself! Surprise! Photo Booth uses your Mac's built-in webcam to take still pictures or video. It also includes a range of goofy effects (click on Effects to see them). Go ahead and have a little fun taking pictures by clicking the camera button. Don't worry if they're embarrassing - we'll talk about deleting files in a little bit!

TIP: *See the green light in the top center of your monitor? That lets you know that your webcam is running.*

Now that you're successfully running your first Mac app, let's talk about how to manage it. In OS X El Capitan, you'll use two areas of the screen to handle your application. First, and most obvious, is the application window itself. In Photo Booth, this is the window where you found the effects and hopefully took a picture or two. Second, you'll use the application's menu bar to get to basic commands and options.

Inside the application window, in the top left corner, you'll see little red, yellow and green buttons. The red button will close the window (like the red X in Windows), and the yellow button will minimize it. The green button will send the application to a full screen display or to a Split Screen view.

So let's take it for a spin! Click the yellow **Minimize** button. Notice how Photo Booth shrinks down to your Dock? Every time you minimize something in El Capitan, it's sent to your Dock. Maximize Photo Booth again by clicking the active Photo Booth icon in your Dock. Try clicking the green **Full Screen** button to see how an application looks while running in Full Screen. To exit full screen, move your mouse to the top left corner until the buttons reappear. Click the green button again to exit Full Screen.

Now, let's look at the top left menu bar at the very top of your screen, outside the Photo Booth application window. See where it says "Photo Booth" in bold? You'll also see **File, Edit,**

View, Camera, Window, and **Help.** These menus change depending on what application you're using. You can also minimize the window from here. Click **Window,** and then **Minimize.**

NOTE: *From here on out, when we talk about consecutive clicks through menu items, we'll write them like this:* **Window > Minimize.**

Do you see how the window itself is minimized, but the Photo Booth menu bar is still displayed at the top of the screen? Use the menu bar to quit the program by clicking **Photo Booth > Quit Photo Booth.** You'll need to get into this habit. In many El Capitan applications, you can close an application window without exiting the application itself. Imagine that you're working on three Microsoft Word documents. If you close all three documents, you're still running the application Microsoft Word, and you'll need to use **Word > Quit Word** to fully exit.

Deleting Files

Now, reopen Photo Booth by clicking on the icon in the Dock. Go ahead and delete any pictures you don't want to keep by clicking on the thumbnails in the bottom part of the screen, and then using the little black x that appears in the corner.

TIP: *you'll see that little black x throughout El Capitan. It almost always means "delete."*

More on Full Screen Applications

We've already practiced using the new green Full Screen button, but there are a couple of other ways to enter Full Screen. In the menu bar, click **View,** and then **Enter Full Screen.** You can also use the keyboard shortcut ^ + ⌘ + F. When an app is in full screen, you can easily navigate between it and your desktop thanks to the three-fingered swipe to the right and left. Take a few minutes to practice swiping between the full screen Photo Booth window and your desktop.

To exit Full Screen, simply press the **ESC** key in the top left of your keyboard, or move your mouse to the top of the screen to recall the menu bar. Use either the blue square in the right corner or **View > Exit Full Screen** to exit.

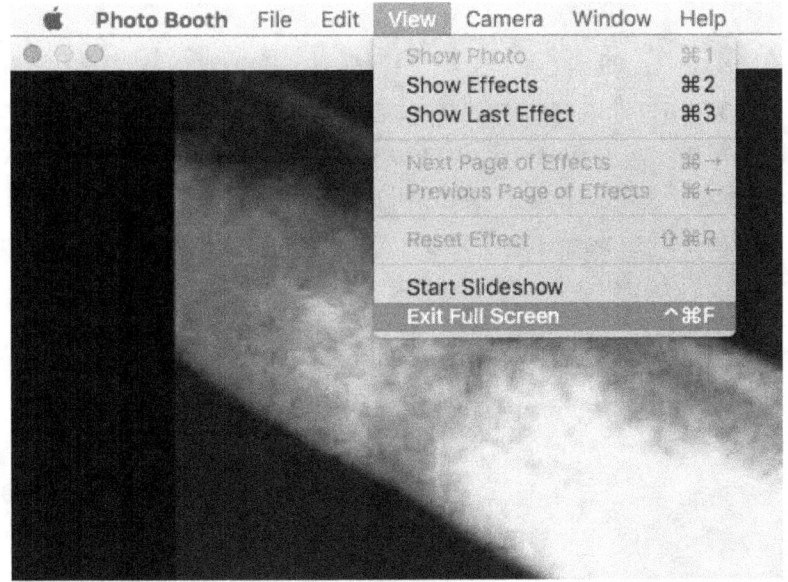

Sharing from Applications

One more thing to notice in Photo Booth: see that little box with an arrow coming out of it right above the thumbnail gallery view? You'll see it in your applications and even in your Finder window. You can share through email, Twitter, Flickr and more, depending on the accounts you've set up, which we'll get into later (**3.1**). It's a handy connectivity feature in the age of social networking!

Before you close Photo Booth, look through the menu bar to see what else you can do! Feel free to open some of the other applications on your Dock as well – don't worry if you don't understand everything yet. Don't forget to practice closing each application using the menu bar.

2.5 Getting Around Using Finder

Now that you've got a general idea about how to run applications, let's talk about file management. Chances are, you have lots of pictures, documents, movies and other files that you'd like to store on your Mac. If you used Migration Assistant during setup, those files may even be in place already. In order to find them, you'll use Finder, the Mac equivalent of My Computer or Windows Explorer.

Finder is the default menu bar you'll see at the top of your screen. You can also open Finder from the Dock. Look for the smiling puzzle piece and click on it.

This will open a **Finder window**. You can open as many Finder windows as you like (this is useful if you need to copy or move files from one folder to another).

Let's take a look at the anatomy of a Finder Window. You should be seeing something like this on your screen right now:

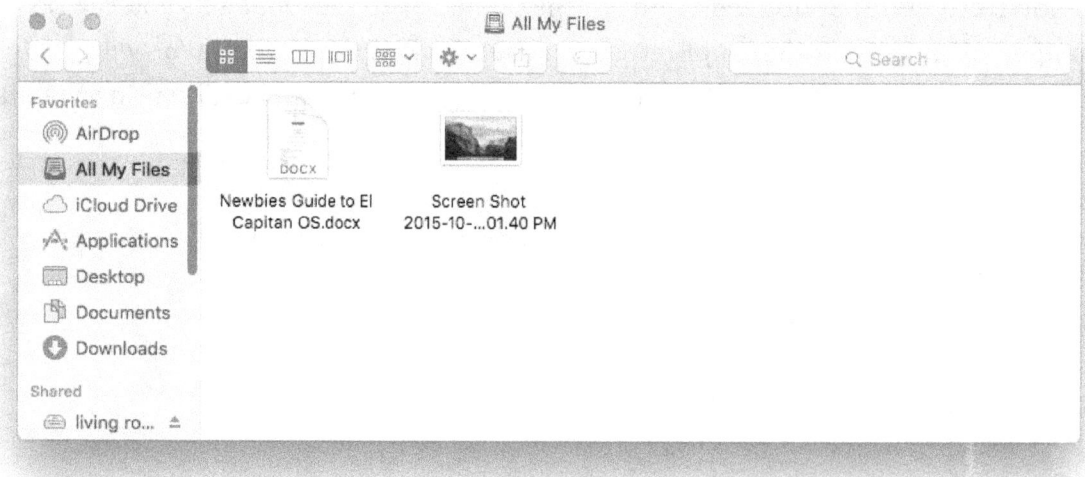

The Finder window includes the red, yellow and green buttons we saw earlier in Photo Booth for closing, minimizing and sending the window to Full Screen. At the top center, you'll see current location displayed in Finder. In the top right corner, there's a Spotlight search field to make finding files and folders easier.

Views in Finder

There are four ways to view folders on your Mac - icons, lists, columns and Cover Flow. Different views make sense for different file types, and you can change the view using the View options icons (pictured above).

Cover Flow View

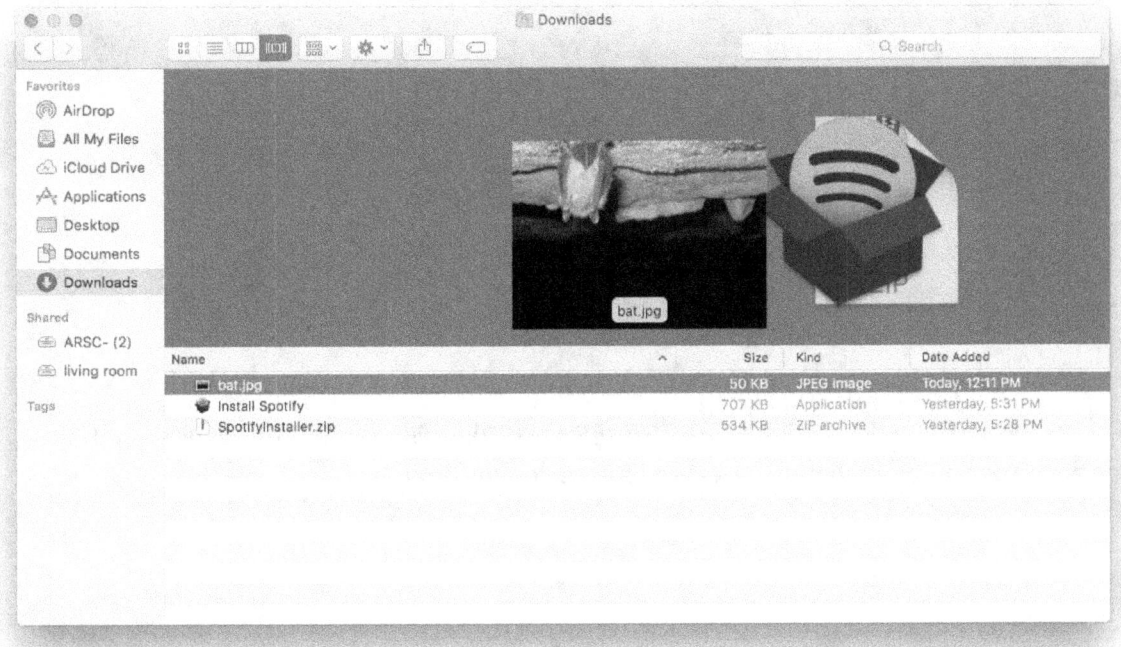

In this example, the view is set to "Cover Flow," as indicated by the icon selected at the top (similar to "Film Strip" in Windows). This is great for looking through pictures or music albums when you need a slightly larger size than icon view gives you. You can also sort files in this view by clicking on the column headers beneath the cover flow display.

Icon View

Icon view can help if you need to sort through several image files or applications. It gives you either a thumbnail of each picture or an icon for each file or app.

List View

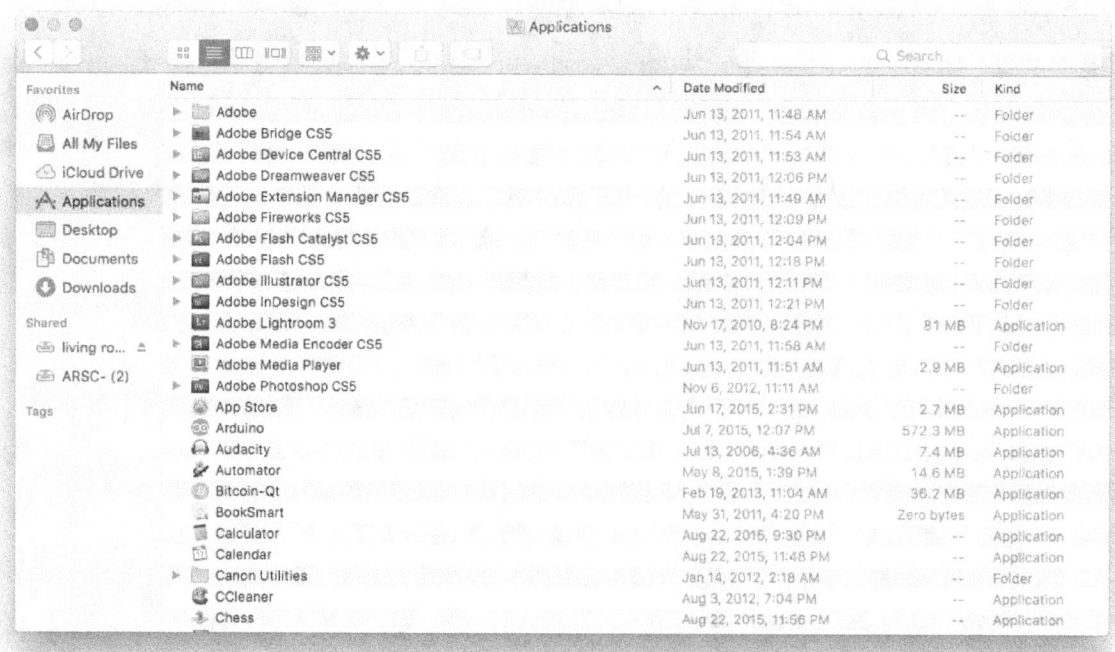

List view, on the other hand, gives you more information about the file, including the date it was last modified. This is a great view for sorting. While you can sort in any view using the sort options button, in list view you can also sort files by clicking the column headers ("Name," "Date Modified," etc.).

Column View

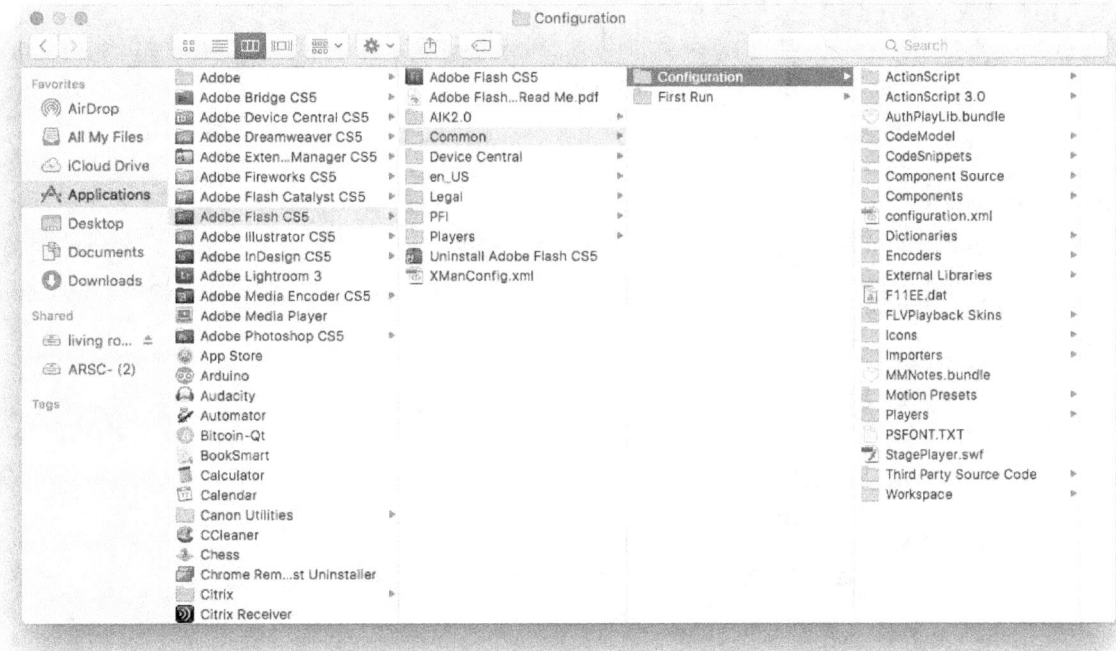

Finally, column view is great when you need to see a file's path. It shows the folder hierarchy a file is located in. Notice that Finder doesn't include the Windows "go up one level" button – Column View is a good way to get the same results and navigate easily through your file structure.

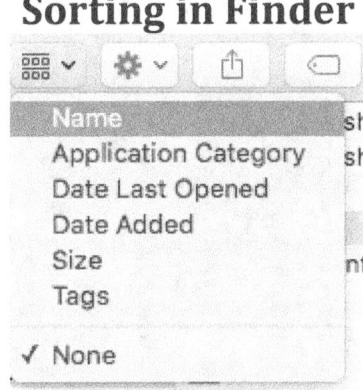

Finder gives you a number of ways to sort your files and folders. You can sort by name, type, application required for opening the file (like Microsoft Word, for example), the date the file was opened, modified, or created, the file size, and any tags you may have applied. This is a handy feature if you're looking for something specific – that giant image file your sister sent you last month, or the spreadsheet you were working on a few minutes ago. You can also sort by clicking column headers if you're in List view.

File Management

Most file management tasks in OS X are similar to Windows. Files can be dragged and dropped, copied, pasted and cut. If you need to create a new folder, use the gear icon in Finder, which will give you the option you need.

El Capitan also allows you to batch rename files, saving you potentially hours of time, depending on your file system. To take advantage of this, select the files you'd like to rename (hint: use COMMAND + click to select multiple files, or use COMMAND + A to select everything). Then right-click the selected files and choose "Rename X items."

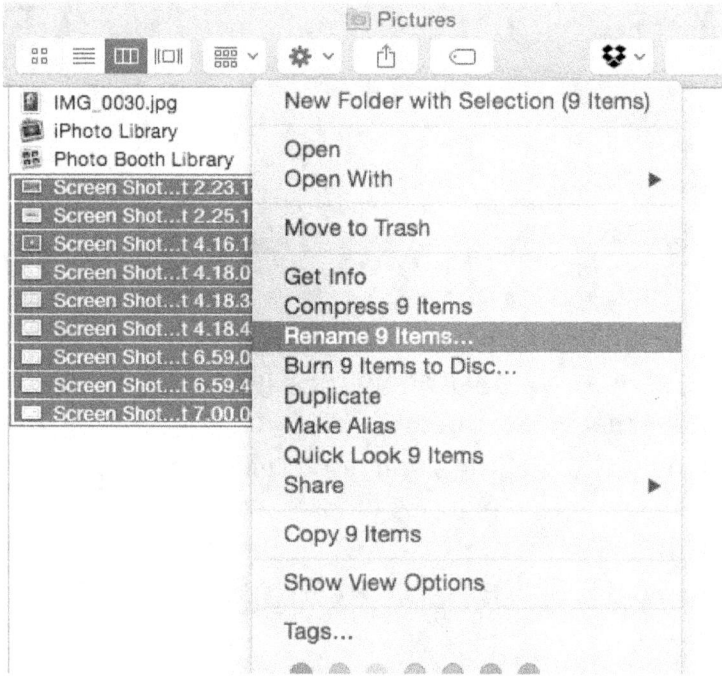

You'll then have the option to replace text or to add text to the file names.

Favorites

If you look on the left side of the Finder Window, you'll see a Favorites sidebar. This section includes high-frequency folders, like Documents, Pictures, Downloads, and more. It also includes "All My Files," which is exactly what it sounds like! El Capitan also includes access to iCloud Drive, which we'll talk about it more detail in **2.6**.

You'll also see your Applications folder in your Favorites panel. Go ahead and open it up. Every application on your computer doesn't have to take up valuable screen real estate on your Dock. If you install an application and don't add it to your Dock, your applications folder is one way to find it and open it (though we do think Launchpad is a faster method – more on this soon!).

To add an application or file to your Favorites menu, just drag it over to the Favorites area and drop it. To remove an item from Favorites, right-click it and select **Remove From Sidebar.**

Spotlight

Spotlight is OS X's search tool, and it's received a massive upgrade in El Capitan. You'll find the Spotlight search field throughout OS X, but it's most obvious inside Finder windows and in its permanent position in the menulet bar in the top right of the screen.

Spotlight now searches not only your files and applications, but also the Internet, using Microsoft's Bing search engine, local movie times, iTunes and the App Store and more. It will also give you results for weather, stocks, sports, online videos and your nearest public transit station. It's never been so easy to search your Mac and the world at large, at the same time.

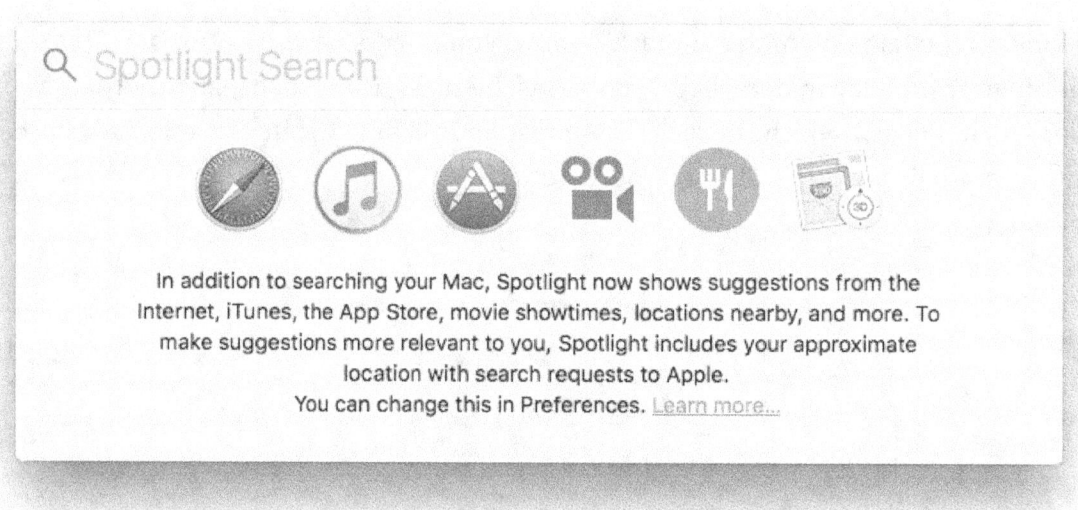

You'll see the Spotlight icon – a magnifying glass – up in the top right corner of El Capitan. Click it to bring up the search box. Type in your search to get started.

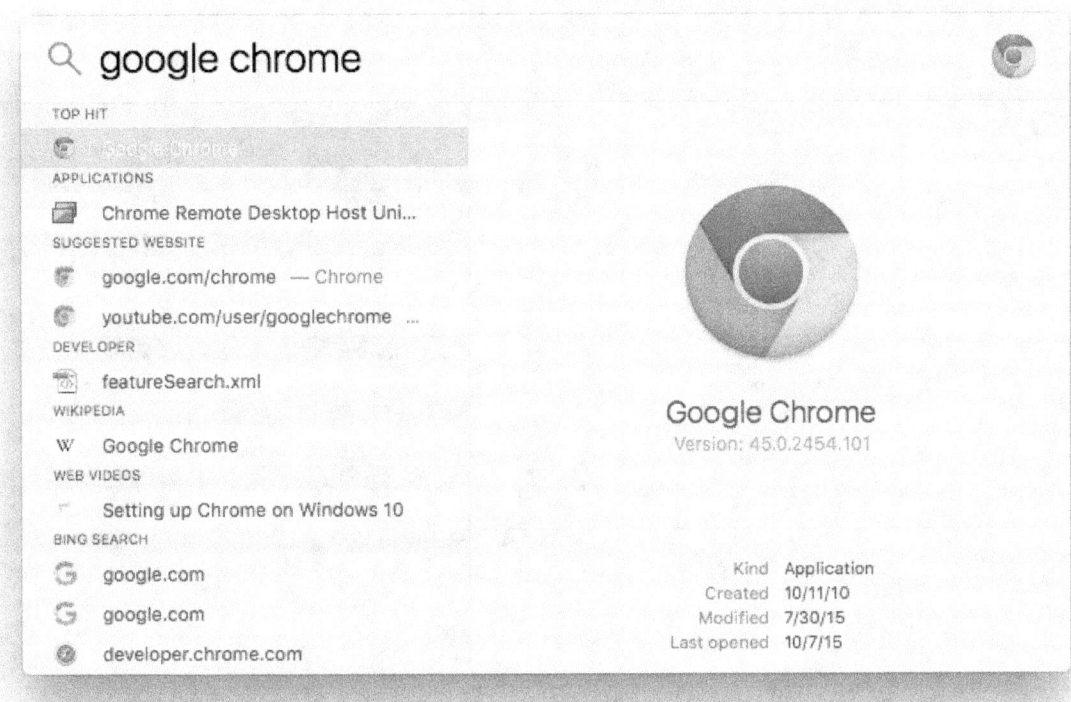

You'll see a menu of search results broken down by location on the left. In the search above, we've retrieved results from the Internet and from our Applications folder.

In our experience, Spotlight is by far the easiest way to find applications and files that aren't on your Dock or your Desktop. One of the fastest ways to get to Spotlight is to memorize its keyboard shortcut - ⌘ + SPACEBAR.

Tabbed Browsing

OS X allows tabbed browsing in Finder windows – it's a handy feature that can keep your workspace a little less cluttered. To open a second Finder tab, press COMMAND + t, or click **File > New Tab**. This will allow you to have multiple Finder windows open inside one frame. This can be quite useful if you need to look at a couple of different Finder screens, but you may still prefer multiple Finder windows for dragging and dropping tasks.

Of course, even with this feature, you may accidentally find yourself drowning in open Finder windows. If this happens, it's easy to consolidate everything. Just click **Window > Merge All Windows** in the Finder menu bar to bring everything together.

Tags

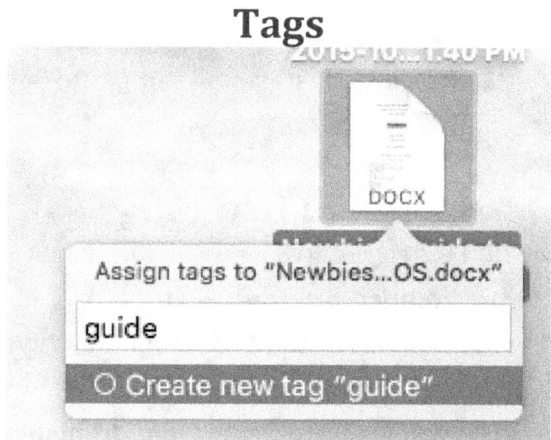

You can also tag your files and folders inside Finder to make them easier to find later. You'll find your tags in the left menu in Finder. There are several default color tags, as well as Home, Important, and Work. To assign a tag, simply right click a file or folder and then click the tag you'd like to use. If you'd like to assign a new tag, right click the item, click tags, and then type the name of your new tag in the white box. After you create a new tag, you can use it again and again, and it will appear on the list of tags (you may need to click **Show All** to reveal it). This is a great way to keep yourself organized, especially with projects that may have files scattered throughout your content libraries.

2.6 Other Need-to-Know Applications and Features in El Capitan

Now that you've got the hang of running applications and managing files and folders in OS X El Capitan, let's cover some other basics.

Launchpad

Launchpad is the rocket ship icon right next to the Finder puzzle piece on your Dock. Go ahead and click it. You're now looking at a list of all the applications stored on your computer in a very simple grid view. We think it's a lot easier to get to Launchpad than it is to navigate to the applications folder in Finder, and even easier to use a five-finger pinch gesture to bring it up (see **2.3**). The Launchpad aesthetic will probably also remind iPad, iPhone and iPod users of their mobile devices (and this isn't coincidental). Every application you download is automatically added to Launchpad.

You can arrange your Launchpad however you'd like by clicking and holding icons and moving them around. You can see how many screens there are in your Launchpad by looking at the series of dots at the bottom. There are four screens in the Launchpad screen shown above – again, this design element is very similar to home screens on iOS devices.

To move between screens, use two fingers to swipe left and right. For a review of swiping, check **2.3**. Serious app users can use the Spotlight search box at the top of Launchpad to find an app quickly, no matter how many others are installed!

Mission Control

Mission Control is located next to Launchpad on the Dock of users who upgraded from older versions of OS X. If you don't see the icon, though, you can still use three fingers to swipe up. Mission Control lets you see everything you have running and makes it easy to switch apps and navigate between full screen apps.

In the Mission Control screenshot below, the user is running Safari in full screen mode, with iTunes, Microsoft Word, a Finder Window and Calendar running on the Desktop. Switching to any of these apps is as simple as clicking on it!

Notice how the Dashboard, Desktop and Safari appear in three separate squares at the top of the screen? These are called Spaces, and you can navigate between them by swiping right and left with three fingers. In El Capitan, the Spaces bar is minimized by default in Mission Control. To view it, just move your mouse over the collapsed Spaces bar. This small tweak gives you more room to view your app windows on the Desktop and cuts down on clutter. You can also quickly take an app into full screen mode by dragging it from the Desktop to the Spaces bar. Similarly, you can bring a full screen app back to the Desktop by dragging it down from the Spaces bar.

One of El Capitan's most exciting features is Split View, which allows you to run two apps in full screen side-by-side, essentially viewing two Spaces at once on your screen. To activate Split View, click and hold the green full screen button in the top left of an app's window. This will cause half of your screen to glow blue. Drag and drop the window onto either half of the screen. Then, click the app window of the second application you'd like to view, and enjoy the Split View experience! Note that some third party applications like older versions of Microsoft Office are not compatible with Split View.

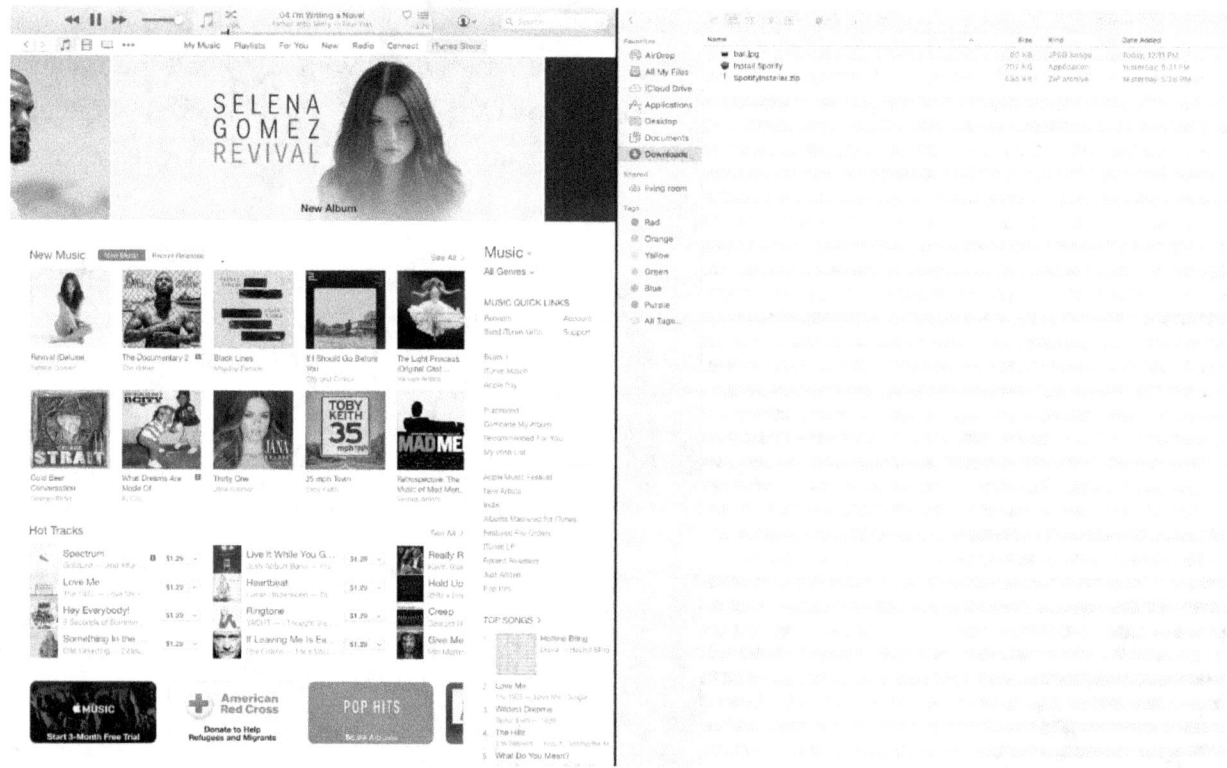

If you'd prefer one Split View window to take up more space than the other, you can simply drag the black dividing line to the right or left to adjust the split.

To exit Split View, simply click the green full screen button on one app. This will cause both Split View apps to revert to Desktop windows.

Safari

Speaking of Safari, the OS X El Capitan upgrade has given Apple's proprietary web browser lots of fixes and features, making it faster and easier to use than ever.

Apple also claims that OS X El Capitan Safari is faster than both Google Chrome and Mozilla Firefox (two popular free internet browsers) and can be used up to two hours longer while running on a MacBook battery. Furthermore, El Capitan includes native Netflix support, meaning Netflix performance is unbeatable and it's not as hard on your battery as it can be in other browsers.

Safari is very easy to use, especially if you have experience with any standard web browser. The Safari browser features forward and backward navigation, represented by the two arrows in the top left corner. Next to the arrows, you'll see the sidebar icon, which reveals your Safari bookmarks, reading list and shared links (more on all of this soon). In the center of the menu bar, you'll find the integrated search/address bar called the Smart Search bar. You can type in search terms ("kittens," "new Belle and Sebastian album," etc.) or website addresses (www.apple.com) here. In the top right corner, you'll find icons for sharing and managing tabs.

When you open a new Safari window or tab, you'll see your favorite sites displayed as icons in the main area of the page. Click the toggle in the top right corner to switch to view the sites that you visit the most frequently.

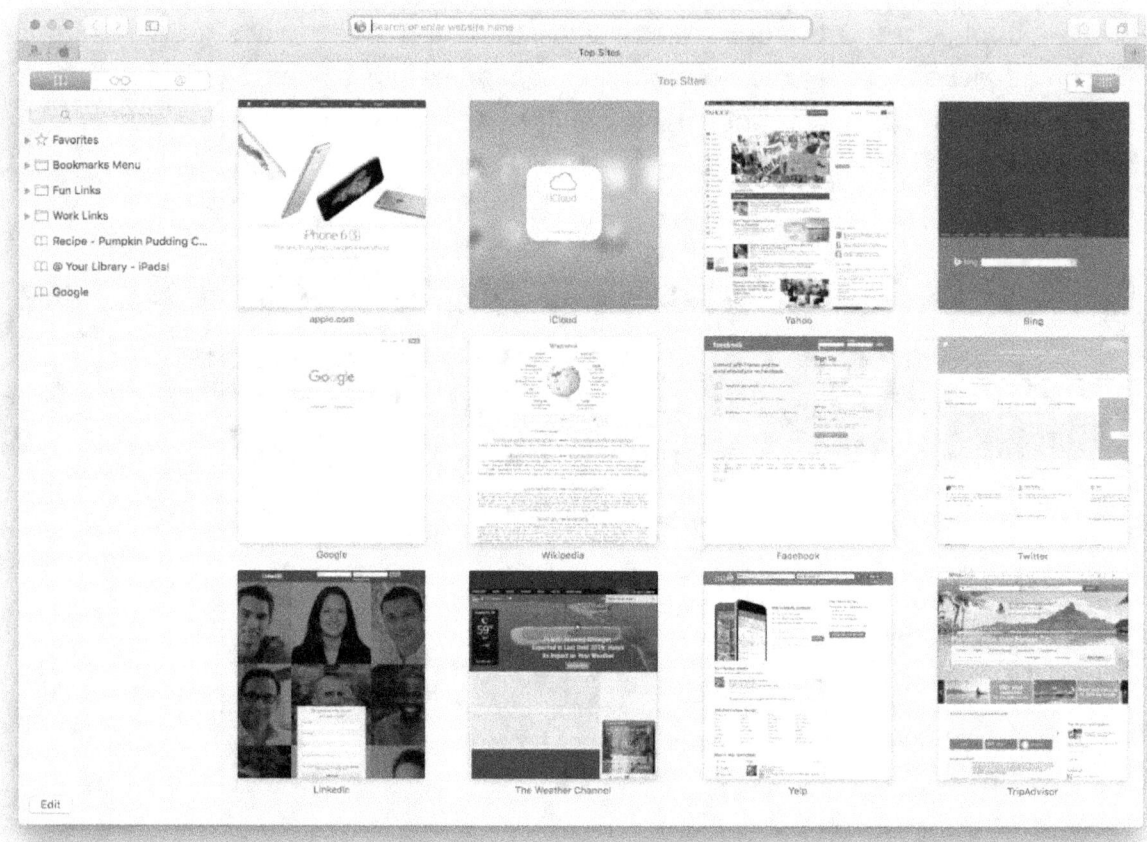

When you click the sidebar icon, a menu with three tabs will appear on the left side of the screen (pictured below). The three tabs are **Bookmarks**, **Reading List** and **Shared Links**. You can add a bookmark using the Share button over in the right corner (also pictured below). You can also add sites to your **Reading List**, which saves the entire site's contents for reading offline (this is a handy trick if you're on a long flight or camping trip with no Wi-Fi access). The **Shared Links** tab will display any URLs that have been shared through Twitter and LinkedIn, if you've integrated these social networks with your Mac (see Part **3.1** for more information).

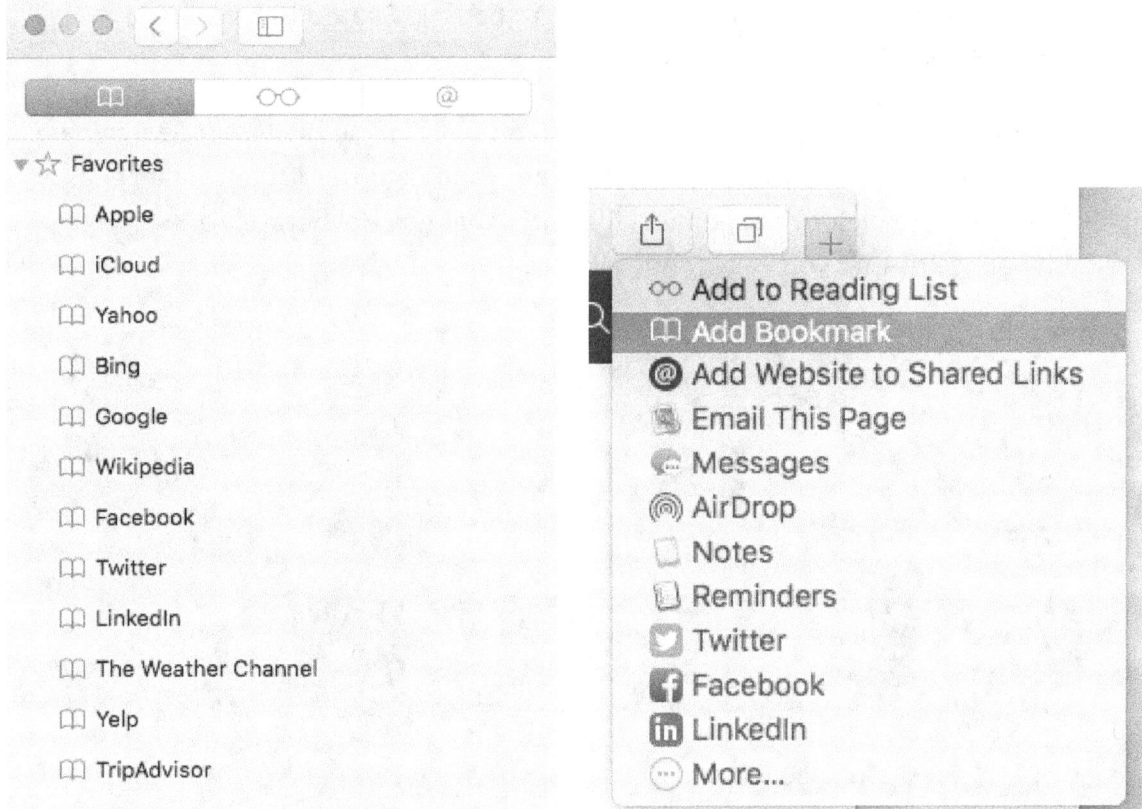

In El Capitan, you can also subscribe to RSS feeds in Shared Links. If you're unfamiliar with RSS, it's basically a way of aggregating new content from your favorite consistently updating sites, like blogs or news sites. If the site's content is published as an RSS feed, you can subscribe by clicking the Share button in Safari and then clicking **Add Website to Shared Links.** If you don't see this in the Share menu, it means that the website doesn't have an RSS feed available.

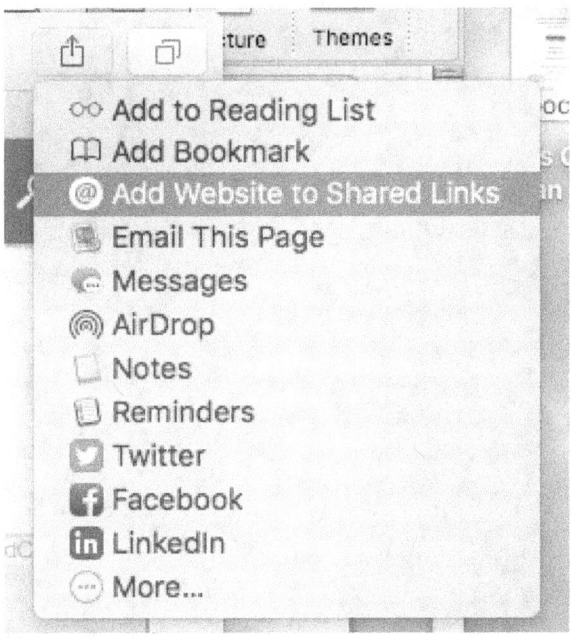

The El Capitan update includes the ability for developers to work with Shared Links to develop Safari extensions. This has a lot of potential to beef up Shared Links' value, especially since RSS is sadly going out of fashion.

Your Favorites folder is easier than ever to get to – in fact, clicking in the Smart Search bar is all it takes to bring it up, just like your iPhone and iPad. Your Favorites list automatically syncs across all of your Apple devices and includes sites that you deliberately add to your Favorites folder and sites that you've recently visited.

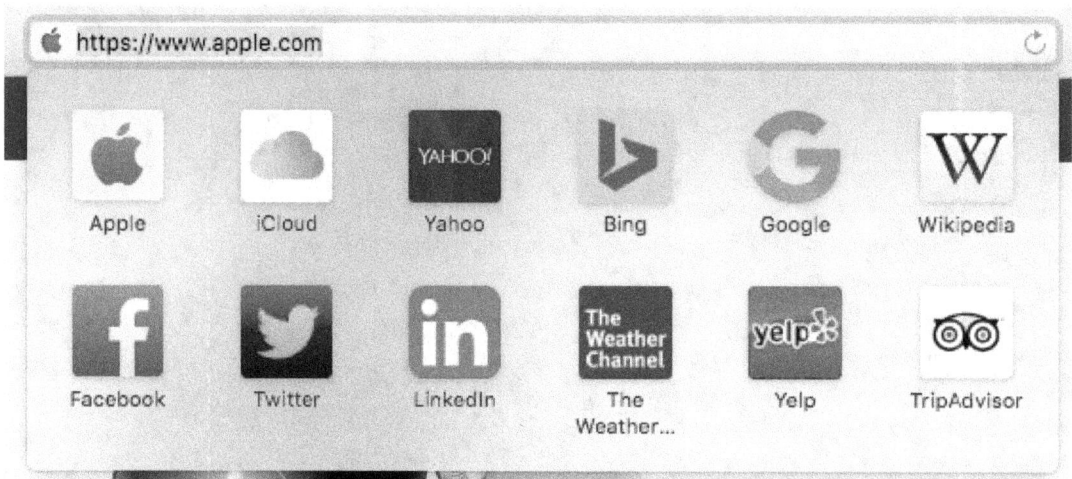

Like every other modern browser, Safari supports tabbed browsing. To add a new tab, either press command + t or click the plus sign at the very far right corner of a Safari window. El Capitan also includes a convenient way to view and manage your tabs, which you can access using the **Show All Tabs** icon in the top right corner. This will show you every tab that you have open, making it easy to navigate your open tabs and find tabs to close. You'll also see every open tab on your other Apple devices, making it exceptionally easy to enjoy continuous browsing, regardless of the device you're using.

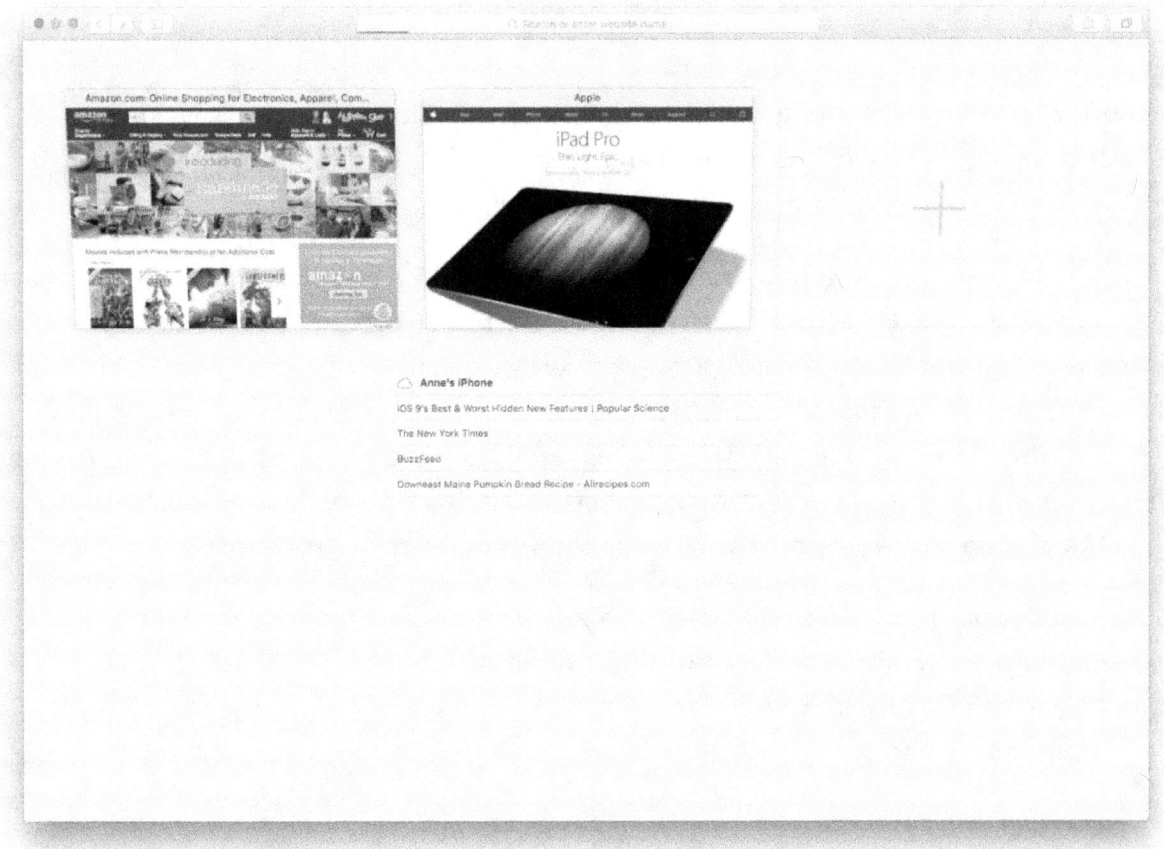

One of our favorite small fixes in El Capitan's Safari is the new audio icon. When a tab plays audio, a speaker icon will appear in the tab, making it easy to see at a glance which of your tabs is making noise. To mute a tab, just click the speaker icon.

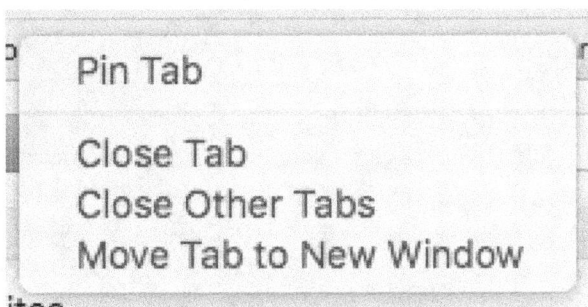

In El Capitan, you can also pin tabs, which can help clean up an overly crowded Safari window. Right click a tab and click **Pin Tab.**

Pin Tab

Close Tab
Close Other Tabs
Move Tab to New Window

Pinned tabs take up less space than full tabs. Below, we've pinned amazon.com and apple.com.

Like OS X Yosemite, El Capitan supports **iCloud Keychain. iCloud Keychain** saves your passwords (always with your permission) and syncs them across all of your devices, so you never have to worry about forgetting a password while you're on the go.

To use iCloud Keychain, be sure it's enabled under **System Preferences > iCloud**. You'll have to set up a security code that you'll use to enable the feature on other Apple devices. Once this feature is enabled, Safari will suggest passwords for you. Of course, the caveat here is that some sites request that passwords not be saved or won't allow Keychain to generate a password. The other possible issue is that you need to be able to remember passwords on other computers that may not run Safari. Nevertheless, it's a useful feature that may save you hours of time that would otherwise be spent on Forgot Your Password? links.

Finally, like its cousins Chrome and Firefox, Safari can host a number of extensions. Extensions provide very specific features that extend the browser's functionality. For example, you can install extensions that will pin to Pinterest for you, block ads or manage your passwords. To find extensions, click **Safari > Safari Extensions...** in the main menu bar.

The App Store

The App Store is The Place for purchasing Mac apps (or finding free ones!). We've put together a list of some of our favorite free apps in **Part 5: The Power of Free,** and most of them are available in the App Store.

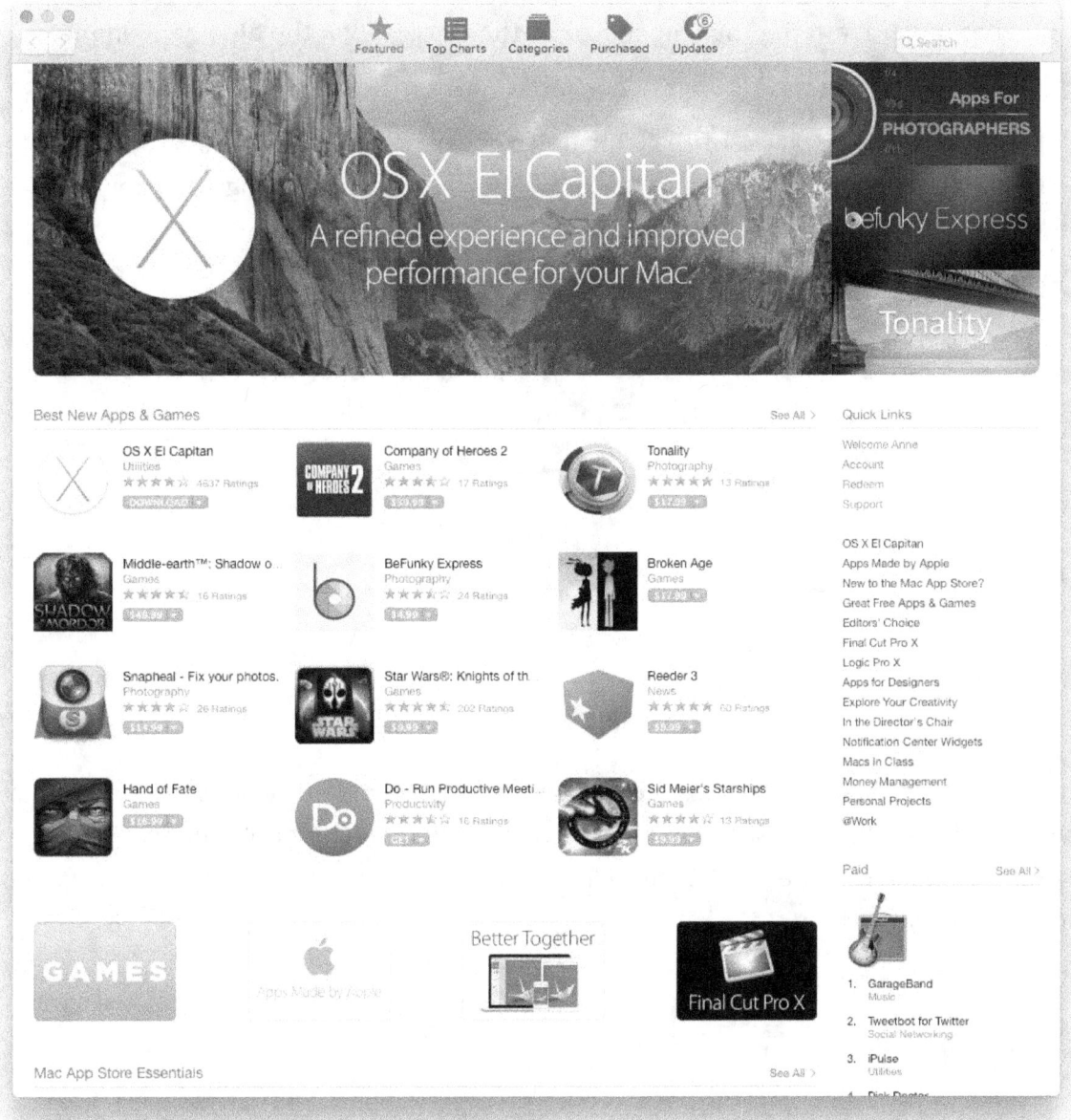

To be clear, not every Mac-compatible program can be downloaded from the App Store. However, many of them can, and the App Store is ridiculously easy to use! Nevertheless, Mac programs can be often downloaded from their creators' websites, unlike iOS apps, which must be purchased through the Apple App Store. Nevertheless, we highly recommend using the App Store to get new apps for your Mac. Apps in the Store must be vetted by Apple, meaning you can trust the safety and quality of your installation. It also means that you'll be notified through the App Store about updates, making it easier to keep everything up to date and running smoothly.

Open the App Store from the Dock. Then search for an app using the search box in the top right of the App Store. When you find an app you'd like to install, click either the word **FREE** or the price next to the app title. Then click **Install**. You'll be prompted to enter your Apple ID and password. You must have an Apple ID to use the App Store.

While your new app is installing, you can keep an eye on its progress by watching the blue progress bar underneath the Launchpad icon in the Dock. When the blue bar completes and disappears, your new app is ready to use!

The App Store also keeps track of available updates for your apps. Generally, new updates will cause a badge to appear over the App Store icon in the Dock letting you know how many updates are available, as seen below.

iTunes

Along with the original iPod, iTunes brought Apple into the media business way back in 2001. Since then, the Apple music world has grown to encompass audiobooks, podcasts, movies, television shows, and more. In El Capitan, iTunes as easy to use as ever and includes a passel of new discovery features.

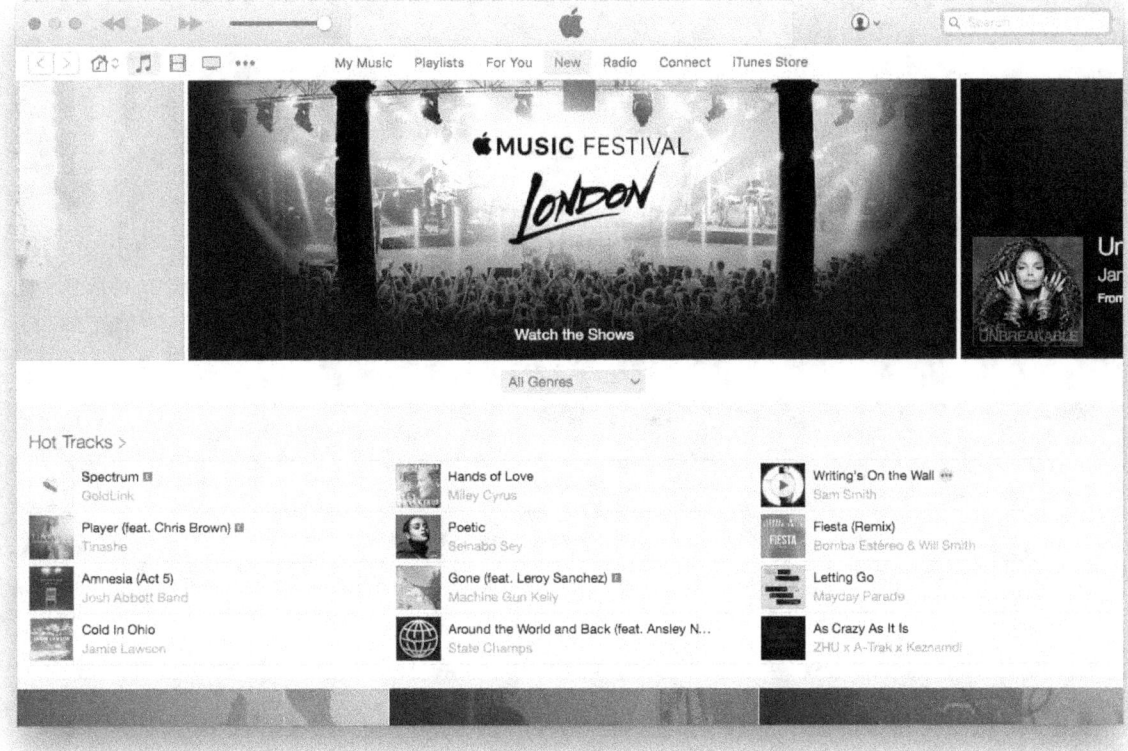

Of course, Apple would prefer that you purchase *all* your music through the iTunes store (accessible from the top left corner of the iTunes media player). Fortunately for those of us with large CD collections, you don't have to. iTunes makes it reasonably easy to import your music. The first time you open the app, you can click **Scan for Media** to locate media files already on your computer.

You can also transfer music from your CD collection to your iTunes library if your Mac has a CD drive. Just insert a music CD and let iTunes do the rest! When asked if you'd like to rip the CD, say yes. iTunes will then analyze the CD and automatically download artist and track information, if you're connected to the Internet. If you'd like to manually enter information for songs, right click them and click Get Info to add artist and album information.

Once your music and movie libraries are set up, you can enjoy them using the playback controls in iTunes under My Music. You can sort your music by song, album, artist, composer or genre in the top right corner of the iTunes window.

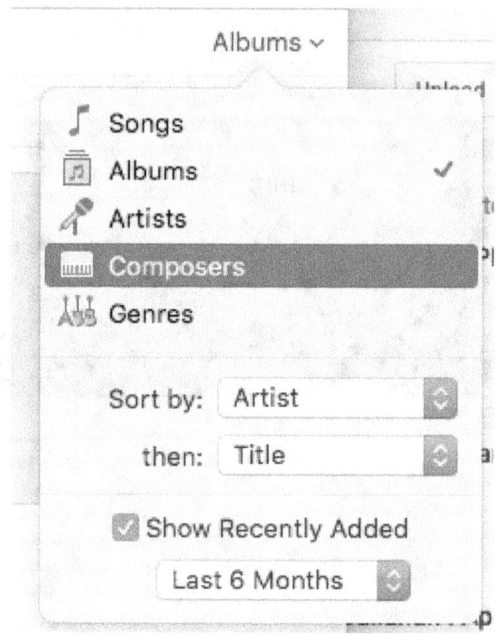

You can also create your own playlists, or rock out to some of Apple's default offerings, which include things like "90s music" and "top twenty-five most played." You can also create Genius playlists. Genius playlists analyze the song that you've chosen to base your playlist on and gather similar songs from your library. We've always been surprised at what an eerily good DJ iTunes can be!

To create your own playlists, click Playlists at the top of the iTunes window. Then, click the plus sign in the bottom left corner. Give your playlist a name, and then start adding music. Drag and drop the songs you'd like to add into the playlist panel. You can always remove them by right clicking them and clicking "Delete." Bear in mind that deleting an item from a playlist does not delete it from your computer.

In OS X El Capitan, iTunes also includes iTunes Radio – a much-loved feature of the iOS version of iTunes. iTunes Radio should have similar streaming radio services like Pandora shaking in their boots. To create a new station, just click the plus sign and enter a song, artist, or genre you want to build a station around. iTunes Radio will then play similar music, keeping track of the songs and artists it selects for you. Of course, Apple makes it very quick and easy to purchase those songs from the iTunes Store, should you choose to do so!

Alongside iTunes Radio, you'll find iTunes Connect, a new iTunes feature that provides a way for fans and artists to connect with each other. iTunes will automatically follow artists in your music library. You'll find their posts in your Connect feed, which might include messages to fans, announcements, pictures and album art, and even preview tracks.

The most recent version of iTunes also includes a three-month trial of Apple Music. Just click **For You** at the top to sign up. Apple Music offers streaming access to over thirty million songs, along with personalized recommendations and tailored live radio. Apple Music costs $9.99 a month for individuals and $14.99 a month for families.

If a large portion of your music library comes from sources other than iTunes and if you have other Apple devices, you may be interested in iTunes Match. It costs $24.99 a year, and will store your entire music library in iCloud. This will allow you to stream your music collection from other Apple devices on demand. This is definitely worth it if most of your music predates your new Apple allegiance!

Photos

The Photos app is built into El Capitan and replaces iPhoto as Apple's most powerful photo manager. If you have a large photo library and/or use an iOS device to take photos, we cannot recommend getting to know Photos strongly enough.

Photos organizes your photo library by date and displays the geographic location the photo was taken (if known). You can also organize your photos into albums by clicking **Albums** at the top. To add a new album, click the + button on the album screen.

The Projects tab is where you can create calendars, cards, prints and more. Select the photos you want to use and tell Photos your shipping address. It's a great way to quickly make personalized gifts for family and friends!

The Photos app also gives you some basic photo editing options, including auto enhancement, rotation, cropping, filters, brightness and color adjustments, spot correction, and the ability to add third party extensions.

You can also add metadata to your photos, including keywords and tags for faces. This is a great way to make your photos easier to search and organize, though it requires some time and consistency to really work well.

Photos also works very well with iCloud Photo Library, and we strongly recommend taking advantage of it. Unfortunately, the free 5 GB of storage iCloud Drive allows disappears pretty quickly for most of us, especially when photos and videos get involved. Extra storage is cheap, though, and it ensures you've always got an online backup of your photo library.

FaceTime

Think an iPhone is the only Apple device you can use to make calls? Think again! Your Mac includes the FaceTime app, which will turn your Mac into a full-fledged videophone. FaceTime is very similar to Skype. It's a great way to stay in touch with friends and family who are far away. Just click on the FaceTime icon in your dock to get started!

The first time you open FaceTime, you'll be prompted to sign in with your Apple ID. You can associate your FaceTime app with a phone number, an email address, or both – whatever you think will be the easiest for your contacts. After everything's set up, you'll see a list of your Contacts (for more on Contacts, see **3.1**). Contacts with FaceTime capability will show a FaceTime camera icon next to their names.

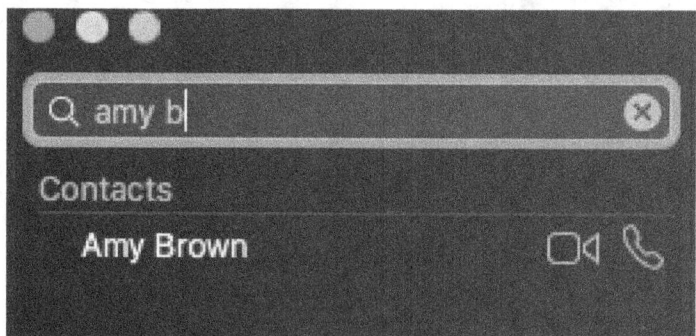

To call someone on FaceTime, just click his or her name (or use the search bar to find them). Then click the FaceTime button to initiate the call. When you're finished, just click the End button in the window.

If you own an iPhone, FaceTime becomes even more useful in El Capitan. If your iPhone is near and connected to the same wireless network as your Mac, you can actually call any number using FaceTime, whether or not that number is attached to an Apple device. Type in the number you'd like to call, and FaceTime will work with your iPhone to make an audio call. iCloud also syncs call history for you, so it's easy to see and return missed calls from your Mac.

iCloud Drive

iCloud Drive was introduced in OS X Yosemite, and it's becoming more and more user-friendly as it matures. iCloud Drive offers wireless file sharing and syncing between compatible devices. iCloud Drive shares files from your apps, including the iWork Suite, as well as any other file type used on your computer or mobile device. It's a little bit like a Mac-specific version of Dropbox. You can monitor which apps are sharing files with iCloud Drive in System Preferences > iCloud > iCloud Drive.

You'll find your iCloud Drive files located in the iCloud Drive folder in Finder. By default, it's listed in your Finder favorites. iCloud Drive files are grouped by the app that they were created in. However, files created outside of native Mac applications can be saved here as well. The files may not be accessible on iOS devices that don't run Microsoft Word, for example, but you can rest easy knowing that your files are safely backed up in the cloud.

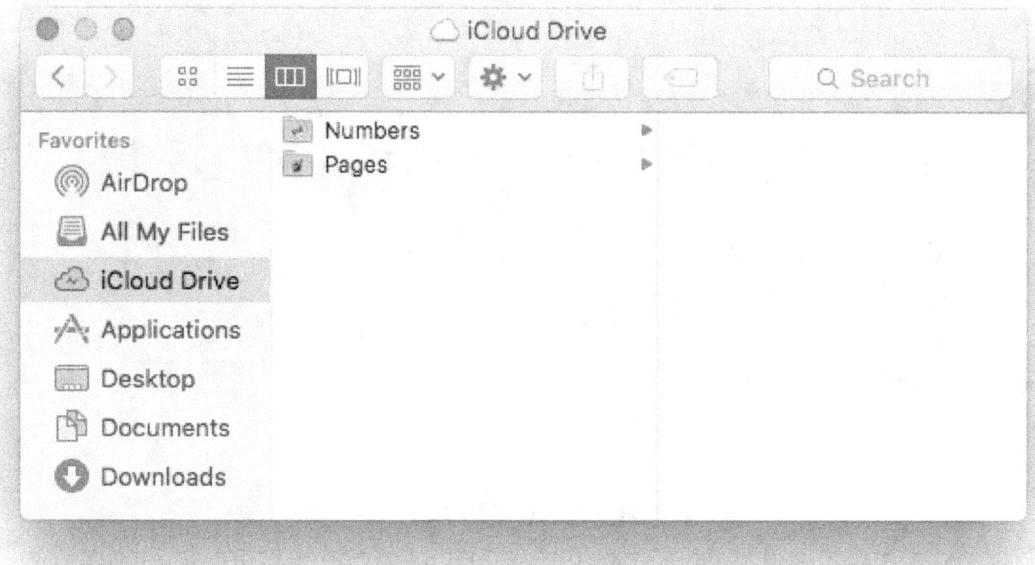

One important thing to be aware of is that your iCloud Photo Library does *not* appear in this folder. Instead, you'll view it through the Photos apps on your Mac or on your iOS devices. Photos definitely count against your iCloud Drive storage limits though, and while every user receives 5 GB of free storage, you may very well need more if you plan to use iCloud Photo Library. At the time of writing, you can purchase additional storage at rates of $0.99 a month for 50 GB, $2.99 a month for 200 GB, and $9.99 a month for 1 TB.

Handoff

Handoff is a great feature that allows you to seamlessly move between your Mac and your iOS devices. Handoff is automatic and works with most Apple apps (Mail, Contacts, Calendar, Safari, Reminders, Notes, Maps, Messages, etc.) as well as with some third party apps.

For Handoff to work, Bluetooth must be enabled on both your iOS device and your Mac (because of technical constraints of Bluetooth, they must also be within 30 feet of each other).

Family Sharing

Family Sharing is one of our favorite OS X features. Family Sharing allows you to share App Store and iTunes purchases with family members (previously, accomplishing this required a tricky and not-entirely-in-compliance-with-terms-of-service dance). Turning on Family Sharing also creates a shared family calendar, photo album, and reminder list. Family members can also see each other's location in Apple's free Find My Friends app and check the location of each other's devices in the free Find My iPhone app or on icloud.com. Overall, Family Sharing is a great way to keep everyone entertained and in sync! You can include up to six people in Family Sharing.

To enable Family Sharing, go to System Preferences > iCloud. Here, click **Set Up Family Sharing** to get started. The person who initiates Family Sharing for a family is known as the family organizer. It's an important role, since every purchase made by other family members will be made using the family organizer's credit card! Once you set up your family, they'll also be able to download your past purchases, including music, movies, books, and apps.

Invite your family members to join Family Sharing by entering their Apple IDs. As a parent, you can create Apple IDs for your children with parental consent. When you create a new child Apple ID, it is automatically added to Family Sharing.

There are two types of accounts in Family Sharing – adult and child. As you'd expect, child accounts have more potential restrictions than adult accounts do. Of special interest is the **Ask to Buy** option! This prevents younger family members from running up the family organizer's credit card bill by requiring parental authorization for purchases. The family organizer can also designate other adults in the family as capable of authorizing purchases on children's devices.

Part 3: Getting the Most Out of Mac

Now that you've got a good grip on how to get around and manage your Mac, let's take a more in-depth look at the features that will help you get the most out of OS X El Capitan. This section will introduce you to the many ways El Capitan will give you more freedom, flexibility, and computing power.

In this section, we'll cover adding and managing mail and social media accounts and contacts, using the other native applications in El Capitan, customizing your machine, managing security and privacy, and a handy list of keyboard shortcuts. This is the section that will help you really make your Mac your own!

3.1 Social Networking, Mail, Contacts and Calendars

OS X El Capitan offers powerful Mail, Contacts and Calendars features to help you get and stay organized. You can synchronize your existing accounts with these native features, and we think you'll enjoy the native app experience much more than web-based mail and calendars!

Adding Accounts

To add accounts, go to **System Preferences** on your Dock (the gears icon) and select **Internet Accounts.** From here, you can add accounts that haven't already been migrated during setup, including iCloud, Exchange, Google, Twitter, Facebook, LinkedIn, Yahoo!, AOL, Vimeo and Flickr. Adding accounts here will start populating El Capitan's native Mail, Contacts, Reminders and Calendar apps, and will add options to your Share button.

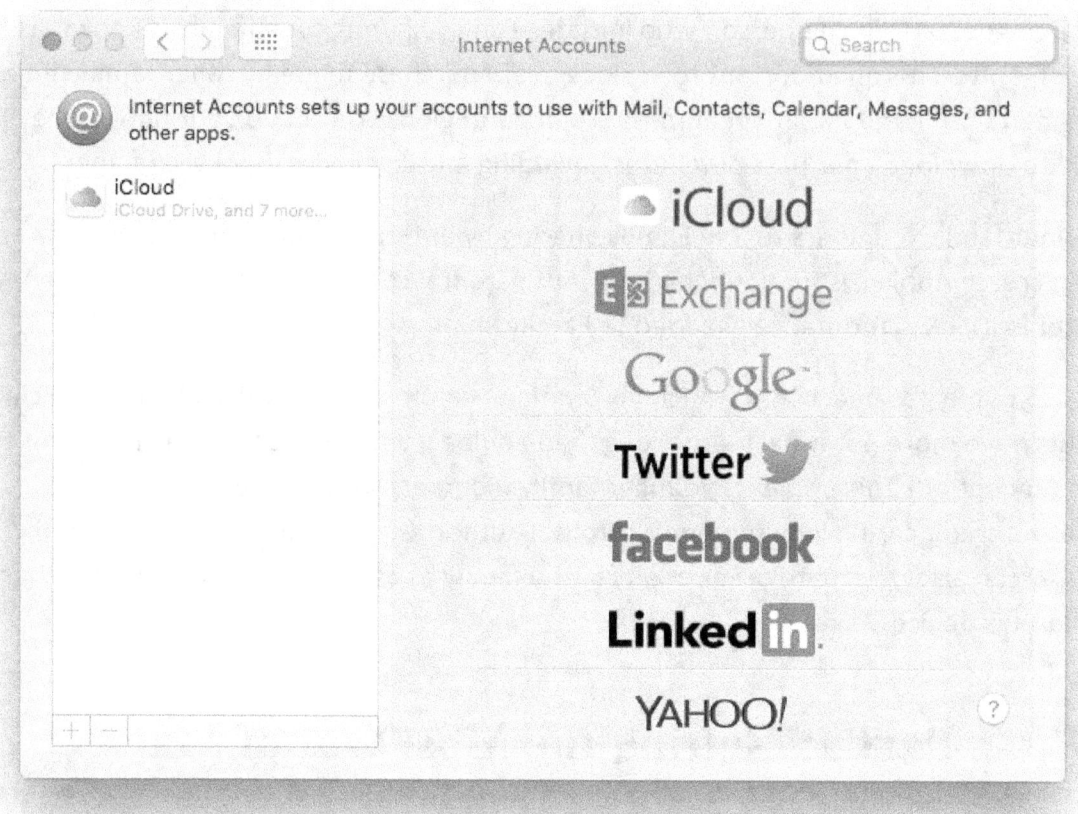

Note: You can also add accounts within the Mail, Contacts, Calendars, and Reminders apps by opening each app and clicking **File > Add Account.** We prefer the System Preferences method because it covers several bases at once!

To add accounts, just click the type of account you'd like to add and enter your login credentials. Follow the prompts to add accounts to the appropriate OS X El Capitan apps.

Once you've added your accounts, you can start using **Mail, Contacts, Calendar, Messages** and **Reminders**, all located on your Dock. If you've enabled iCloud, these apps will all stay synced with their counterparts on your Apple mobile devices. These apps also communicate with your Notifications Center (**3.2**), so that you can keep track of all of your incoming notifications in one unobtrusive spot without needing to open several separate applications.

Twitter, Facebook, LinkedIn, Vimeo and Flickr

OS X El Capitan supports deep Twitter, Facebook, LinkedIn, Flickr and Vimeo integration. To get started, simply sign in to your account(s) from **System Preferences > Internet Accounts**. Select Twitter, Facebook, LinkedIn, Flickr, or Vimeo, and then enter your username and password. From now on, you'll be able to use that account with the Share button throughout El Capitan and receive notifications in your Notifications Center.

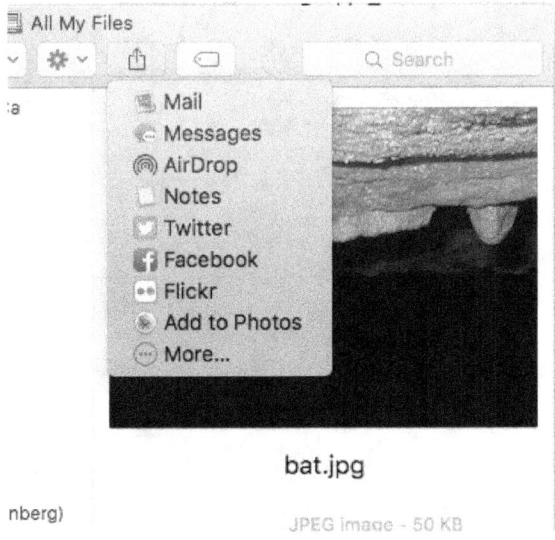

bat.jpg

JPEG image - 50 KB

nberg)

Using Mail

Mail is very easy to use after you've added all your accounts. The Notification Center will help you be sure you never miss another message, and the Mail app will help you organize the daily barrage so that you see the most important messages.

The Mail app will pull in existing folders from your webmail accounts for you. It also gives you the ability to set up VIP senders, like your mother or your boss, so that you don't miss the most important communications.

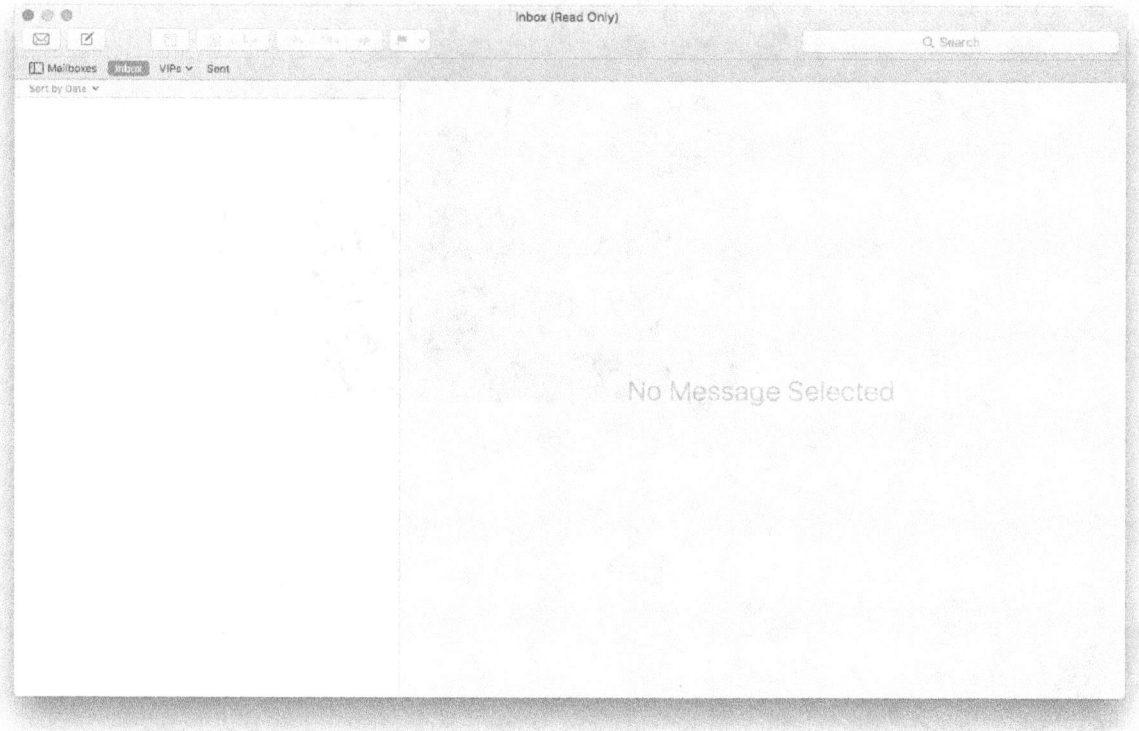

To write a new email, click the new message icon in the top left (it's the square and pencil icon). This brings up the new message screen, where you can enter recipients' addresses, attach files, and of course, write your message. When everything looks good, just click the paper airplane icon in the top left corner.

The Mail Drop feature allows you to send attachments up to 5GB – even if your email service won't allow such large attachments. Markup allows you to annotate images, fill out forms and insert signatures without downloading, editing and re-uploading the attachment. Instead, you can do it all from the Mail client.

The El Capitan update brings a few big and welcome changes to Mail. Composing new messages in full screen is easier than ever, since you can now open a draft in full screen and leave your inbox on the desktop, making it effortless to switch between your draft and your other messages. You can manage multiple drafts in full screen tabs rather than separate windows. The strikethrough button now lives right on the format bar – a small improvement guaranteed to make editors happy!

Mail has also gotten much smarter. It will automatically find contact and calendar information for you and add it to the Contacts and Calendar apps for you. El Capitan also adds the iOS swipe management gestures to Mail. Swipe right on a message to mark it unread, or swipe left to delete it. You can also use natural language to search your messages, making it easy to find every email from last week with an attachment.

Using Calendar

El Capitan's Calendar, like Mail, pulls in your existing calendars from Google, Facebook, and more, so that everything you need to show up for shows up in one location. Calendar will also keep you up to speed with upcoming holidays and Facebook friends' birthdays. Like most other apps in El Capitan, Calendar syncs between El Capitan and all your iOS devices, so you'll always know what's going on.

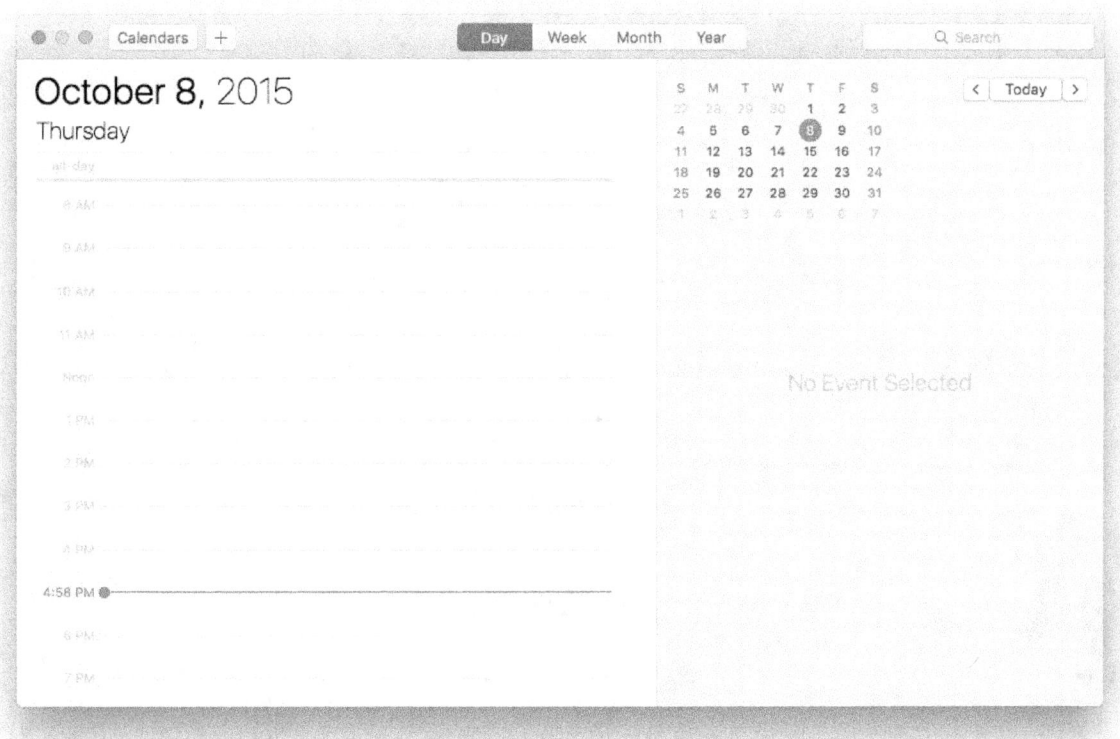

The El Capitan Calendar includes a day view mode that makes it easier to see your daily events. Of course, you can also view your calendar by week, month or year using the buttons in the top center of the Calendar window. In El Capitan, Calendar will automatically create events based on mail messages (for example, flights and hotel stays). Just click **Accept** in these automatically generated events to add them to your calendar.

To manually add a new event in Calendar, click the plus sign in the top left corner or double click the day or time at which you'd like to add the event. From there, you can ad a location for the event, invite your contacts, and add notes, attachments and links. You can also see maps for locations that El Capitan can recognize. El Capitan can even calculate how long it will take you to get to a location. In fact, the El Capitan upgrade includes automatic notifications that let you know it's time to leave for every event with a location. It even factors in current traffic to give you the most accurate travel time estimate possible. You can also see the weather report for a location at the time an event is scheduled, so you'll know what to wear.

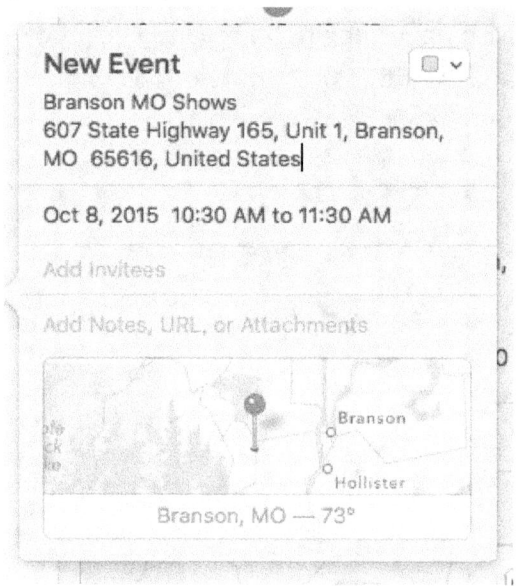

Calendar works with Handoff, and includes a special shared family calendar when Family Sharing is enabled.

Using Contacts

You'll find that many apps throughout El Capitan rely on your contact list, including Mail, Messages, FaceTime, Reminders and more. Contacts can be manually added or pulled in from your synced Internet accounts in El Capitan. We found our Facebook contacts were a little overwhelming, so we used **System Preferences > Internet Accounts** to remove them. Your mileage may vary, of course.

Contacts is very simple to use. Your contacts appear in an alphabetized list, with as much or as little detail as you'd like to add. Like most other apps, you can add new contacts using the plus button in the lower left corner of the Contacts view area, and anything you add will be synced across your Apple device family.

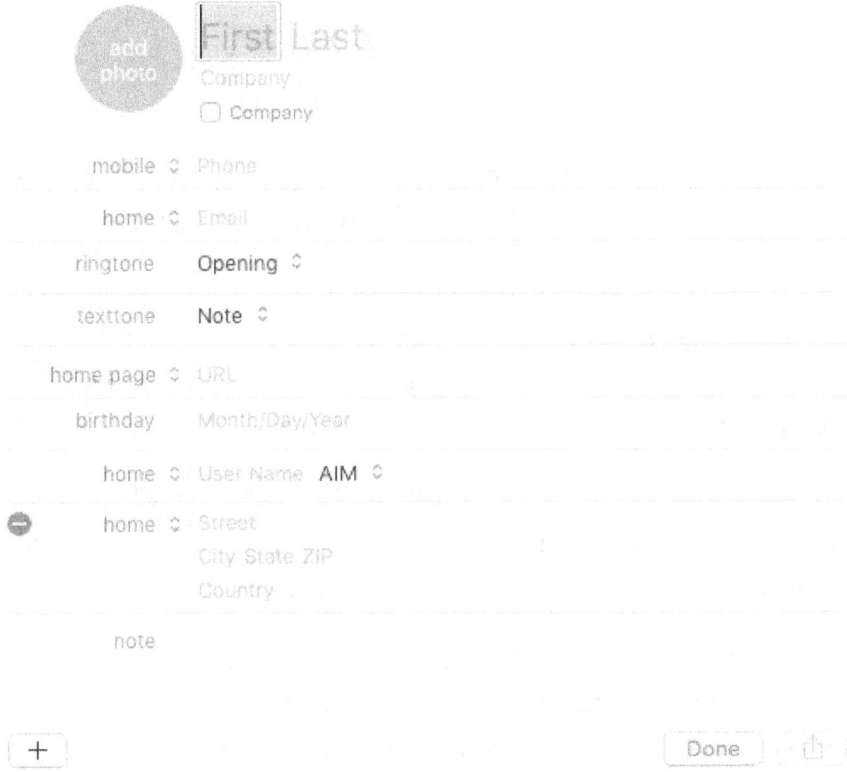

There are quite a few more fields here than it seems at first. Each field with arrows can be changed – for example, clicking "home" next to Email reveals home, work and other, as well as custom.

3.2 Other Native Features and Apps in OS X El Capitan

Notification Center

The Notification Center, located at the top right of your screen, unifies your reminders, calendar alerts, email and social networking notifications, Game Center messages and more.

Notification Center gives you a comprehensive view of what's going on in your electronic life. You can also respond to many notifications in the Notifications Center. When a new message arrives, you can type your reply directly in the notification screen, instead of opening up Messages and doing it there.

You'll find your Notifications Center is organized into two tabs – Notifications and Today. The Notifications tab includes all your recent notifications, grouped by app, while the Today tab gives you an overview of what's going on today and displays the widgets you've enabled.

El Capitan, like its mobile counterpart iOS 9, includes widgets in the Notifications Center. By default, the Calendar, Weather, Stocks, Reminders and Tomorrow widgets are included in the Today tab of the Notification Center, but you can adjust your widgets by clicking the Edit button. You can add the Apple widgets Calculator, Social (Twitter, Facebook and LinkedIn) and World Clock, or you can add third party widgets like Evernote that come with certain app downloads from the App Store. El Capitan also introduces two new widgets – Find My Friends, which allows you to see the location of all of your friends who've connected with you, and iTunes, which gives you playback controls for your tunes built right into the Notifications Center.

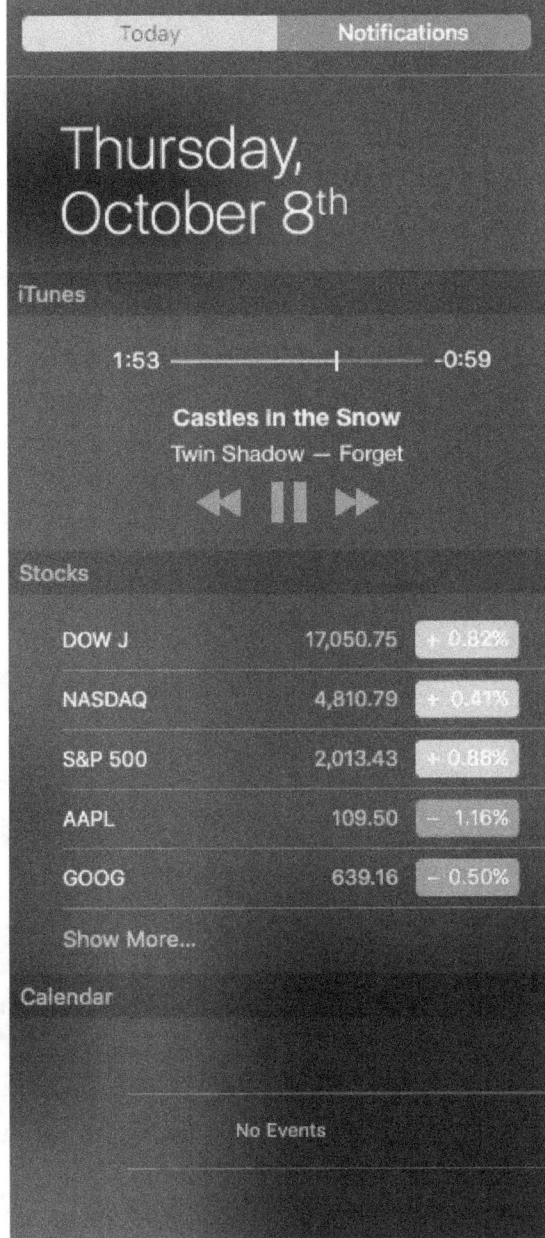

*TIP: Notification Center makes a noise every time a new notification is received. If it's starting to get to you, you can turn off the sound for each notifying app under **System Preferences > Notifications.** You will need to turn off sound for each individual app one at a time.*

Game Center

Game Center is Apple's social gaming network, available in Launchpad or in your applications folder. It lets you connect and play with friends (old and new) online, compete for top spots on leaderboards, and earn public points and achievements. If you have plans to play any social games on your Mac, it's a good idea to set up a Game Center account. If you change or add Mac or iOS devices in the future, you'll be able to keep your game contacts, achievements and high scores in the process.

Not every game available in the App Store is Game Center-enabled, though a large number are, including many of the most popular (Angry Birds, Plants versus Zombies, Clash of Clans, et al.). If you've enabled iCloud on your Mac and your mobile devices, you can use Game Center to stay in sync with your mobile gaming without plugging anything in. You won't be able to play your iOS games on your Mac, unfortunately. However, a number of popular games are available in the App Store. Inside Game Center, just click on **Games** and then **Find Games in the App Store**.

Reminders

Reminders help you keep track of things you need to do. They sync with other iCloud-running devices you may use, and can be set up with tasks from Exchange, Google Calendar, and other reminder services. You can set due dates and locations to trigger reminders (meaning you'll receive a reminder either when the due date approaches or when you reach a location, if you've enabled Location Services). You can also check off completed tasks and keep track of everything you've already completed – remember that checking an item off doesn't actually delete it! You can create custom lists that also sync across your iCloud-enabled devices. Reminders is located on your Dock by default.

In El Capitan, Reminders have been added to the standard Share menu, meaning you can create a reminder based on an email message in Mail, a web page in Safari, or a photo in Photos. The update also adds the ability to press snooze on a notification if you're not ready to deal with it.

Reminders works with Handoff, and a special shared Family list appears when Family Sharing is enabled.

Notes

Notes started life as a humble scratchpad application, perfect for jotting down quick messages that could be easily accessed across the Apple device family. However, in El

Capitan, Notes has received some serious attention.

Notes now includes the ability to add photos, maps, lists and more. You can create a new Note inside the Notes app and add multimedia there. Just start a new Note and right click it for the options to import images or add screen selections.

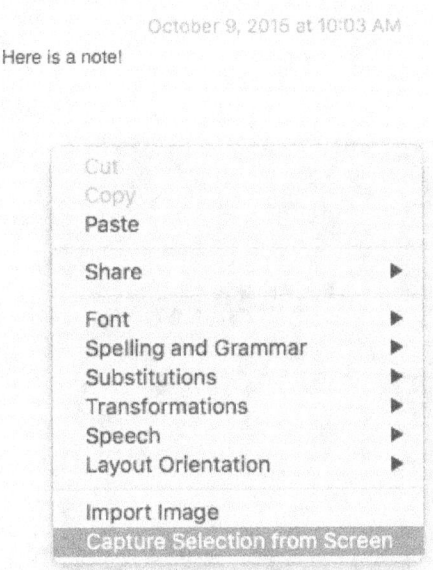

However, the real power of Notes stems from its inclusion in the Share menu throughout El Capitan. You can share web pages, maps, email messages, photos, and more straight to Notes by clicking the Share button. You'll have the option to add content to an existing Note or to create a new one. This is a great way to organize information, whether you're working on a research project or remodeling your house. In the screenshot below, we're sharing a YouTube video to Notes.

You can add all kinds of media to your Notes – maps, videos, PDFs, etc. This is often as simple as drag and drop. For example, in order to save a photo in your Note, just drag it out of Photos and drop it into the Note. Notes even includes an attachment browser so you can easily see all your media. This is a lifesaver when you can't remember exactly which Note you saved that adorable picture of a red panda in!

Notes also includes the ability to create checklists. Just click the Checklist button to transform a plain text list into an interactive checklist. Check off items as you finish them, just like you would on a scrap piece of paper.

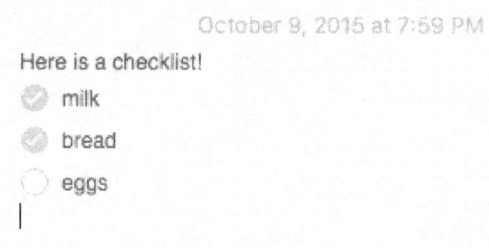

Messages

Messages, formerly known as iMessage, lets you send a message to anyone using OS X Mountain Lion or later, iPad, iPhone, or iPod Touch. If you own an iPhone and it's connected to the same wireless network as your Mac, you can also use Messages to send SMS messages to non-Apple-using friends and family. The first time you open Messages, you'll see the following prompt:

Click **Turn On**. You'll then be given a verification code. Open Messages on your iPhone and type in the code to allow SMS messages through your Mac.

Messages uses the information stored in Contacts. To send a message, click the "New" icon and start typing a friend's name. If your friend is in your Contacts, his or her name will pop up. If not, you can send a message to a phone number or email address. You will need to be logged in with your Apple ID in order for Messages to work.

You can also set up Messages to enable AIM, Yahoo! and Google Talk and do all your instant messaging from one place. Visit **Messages > Add Account** to add additional IM services.

Maps

While you may not navigate with your Mac quite as often as you might with a smart phone or tablet, Apple's proprietary navigational app Maps is still useful for planning a route from home – especially since you can send your routes straight to your iPhone or iPad using the Share button!

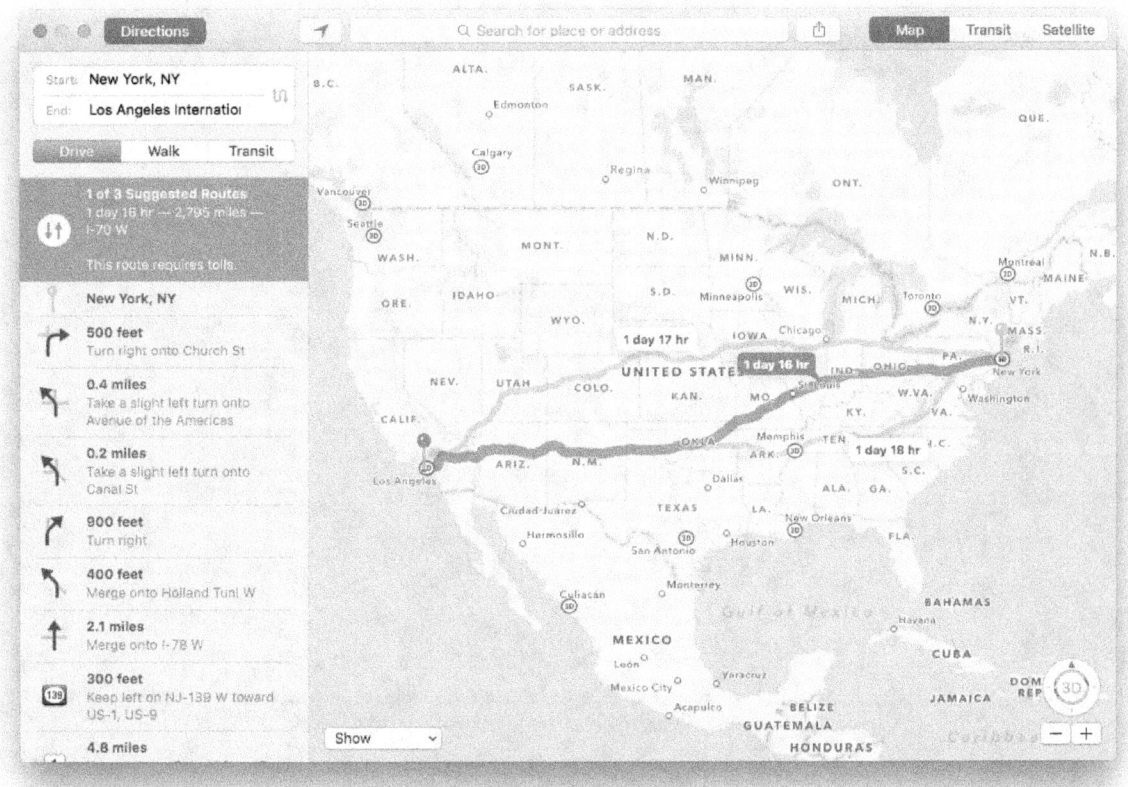

There are a number of other really useful functions in El Capitan Maps. We were really pleased to discover that we could turn a map into a PDF – a portable, offline, and printable file we can move around a little more easily than online mapping services. Just click on **File > Export as PDF** to take advantage of this.

The most exciting addition to Maps in El Capitan is public transit. Now when you ask Maps for directions, you can choose between driving, walking and transit routes. Transit directions give you detailed information about how to navigate public transportation, including route names and schedules. You can also let Maps know when you plan to leave – now, in 30 minutes, in 60 minutes, in two hours, or at a time of your choosing. Perhaps more usefully, you can let Maps know when you need to arrive, and Maps will let you know exactly when you need to get moving.

If you've ever been flummoxed by a busy subway station in an unfamiliar city, Maps can help you prepare by giving you a detailed look at a station, including its entrances and shops. Just zoom in on the station to view it.

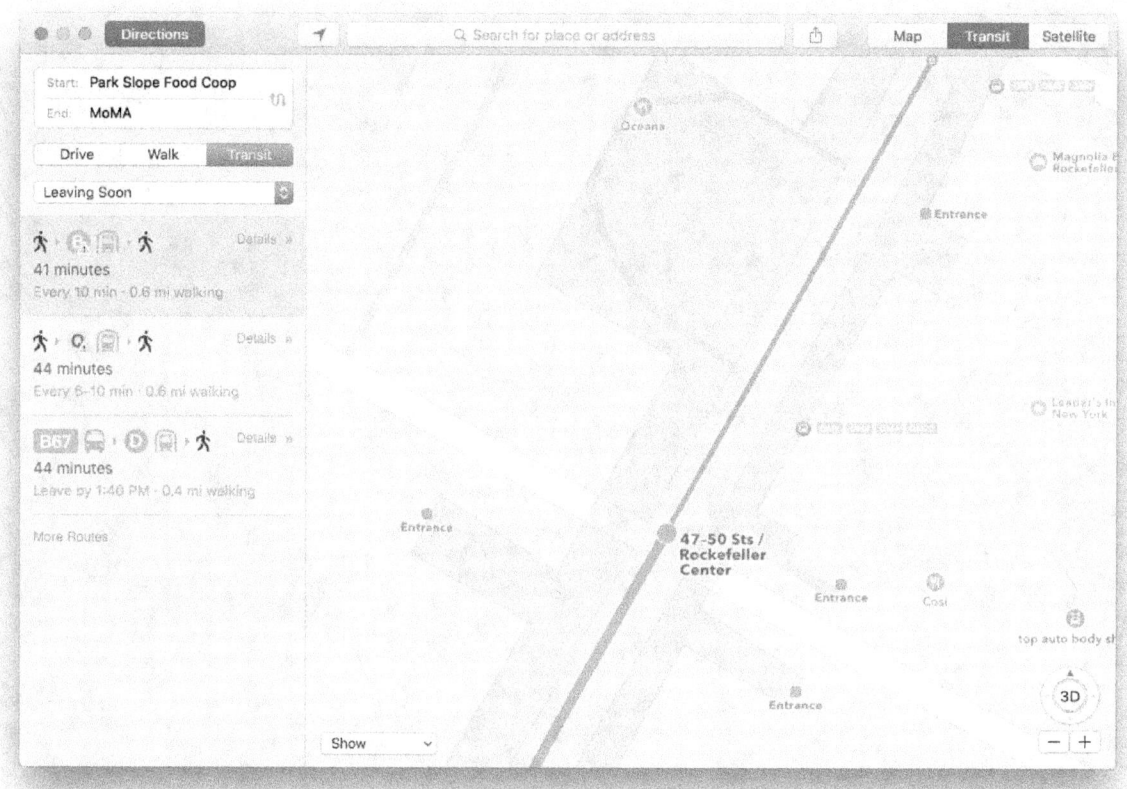

You can also choose to view Maps in Map, Transit and Satellite modes. Map view gives you a standard road map of the area. Transit displays public transportation lines and stops. Satellite gives you a photographic bird's eye view. You can also view a 3D representation of an area (FlyOver, in Apple-speak) by clicking the 3D icon in the lower right corner.

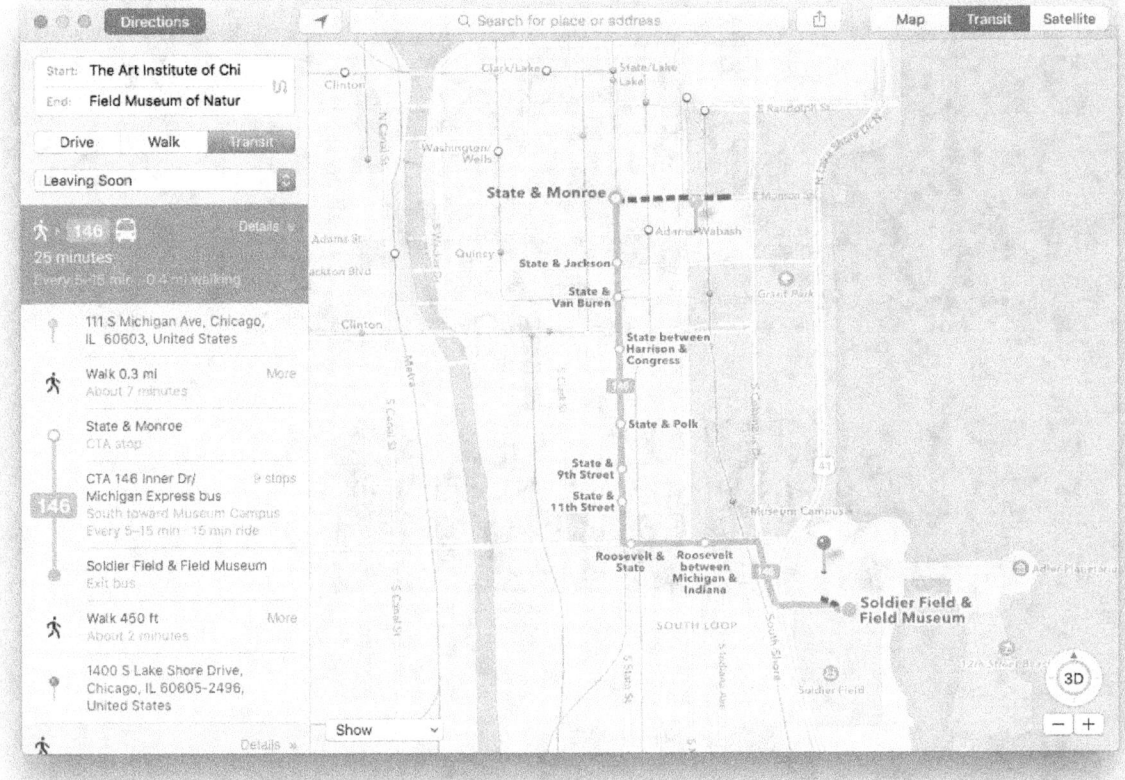

Like the iOS version of Maps, you can save bookmarked locations, see Yelp reviews for public locations, add addresses to your Contacts, and rate locations.

iBooks

iBooks is essentially iTunes for books, and with over two million books to choose from, it's a powerful platform for bookworms.

iBooks works very similarly to iTunes. The app itself displays your personal library with a link to the store in the top corner. In the store, you can choose from bestsellers, free books, and more. You can also use the categories link to find popular titles in your favorite genres.

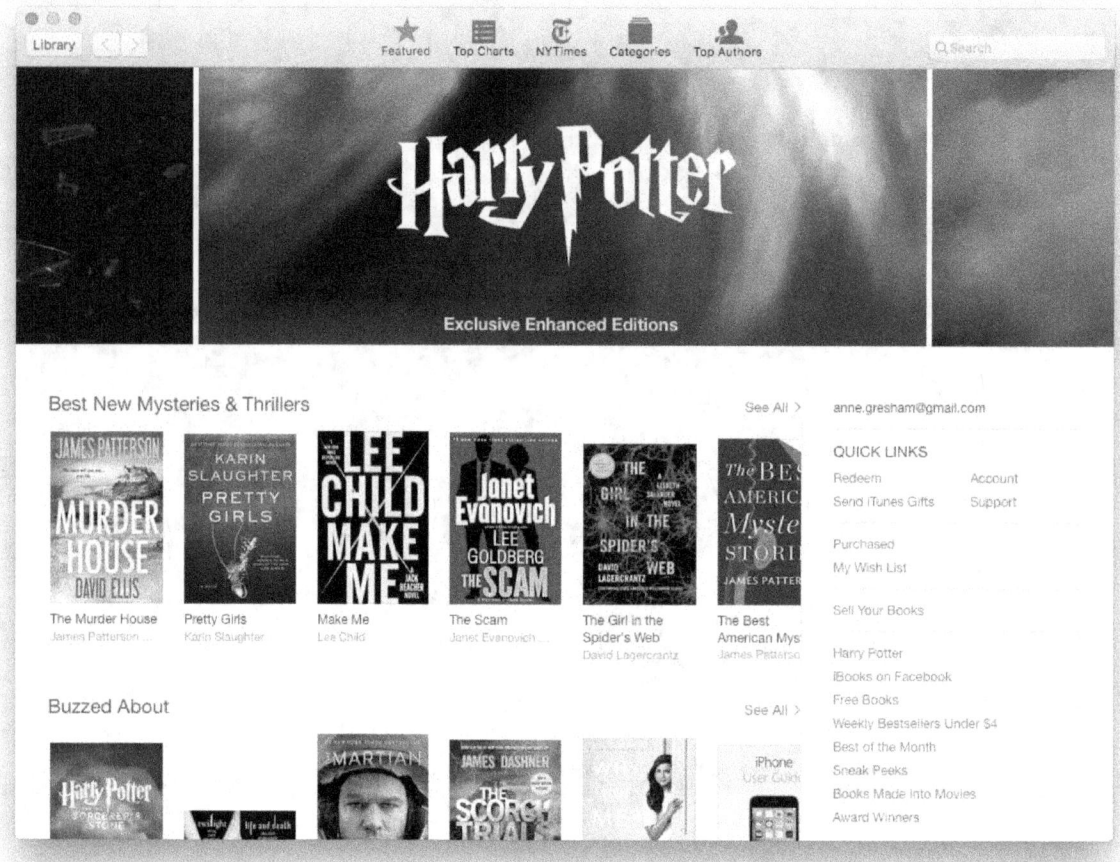

If you've purchased any iBooks titles on other iOS devices, you'll be able to sync them with your Mac. iBooks is also extremely useful for students – it may not be as comfortable to read on a computer screen, but it's certainly much easier to take notes with a full keyboard!

In the screenshot below, you'll see the opening pages of *Alice in Wonderland* by Lewis Carroll. If you look at the top, you'll see basic controls for returning to your library (the book icon), viewing the table of contents, and navigating your notes. In the right corner, you'll be able to adjust the font size, search, and add bookmarks.

to her feet, for it flashed across her mind that she had never before seen a rabbit with either a waistcoat-pocket, or a watch to take out of it, and burning with curiosity, she ran across the field after it, and fortunately was just in time to see it pop down a large rabbit-hole under the hedge.

In another moment down went Alice after it, never once considering how in the world she was to get out again.

The rabbit-hole went straight on like a tunnel for some way, and then dipped suddenly down, so suddenly that Alice had not a moment to think about stopping herself before she found herself falling down a very deep well.

Either the well was very deep, or she fell very slowly, for she had plenty of time as she went down to look about her and to wonder what was going to happen next. First, she tried to look down and make out what she was coming to, but it was too dark to see anything; then she looked at the sides of the well, and noticed that they were filled with cupboards and book-shelves; here and there she saw maps and pictures hung upon pegs. She took down a jar from one of the shelves as she passed; it was labelled 'ORANGE MARMALADE', but to her great disappointment it was empty: she did not like to drop the jar for fear of killing somebody, so managed to put it into one of the cupboards as she fell past it.

'Well!' thought Alice to herself, 'after such a fall as this, I shall think nothing of tumbling down stairs! How brave they'll all think me at home! Why, I wouldn't say anything about it, even if I fell off the top of the house!' (Which was very likely true.)

Down, down, down. Would the fall NEVER come to an end! 'I wonder how many miles I've fallen by this time?' she said aloud. 'I must be getting somewhere near the centre of the earth. Let me see: that would be four thousand miles down, I think—' (for, you see, Alice had learnt several things of this sort in her lessons in the schoolroom, and though this was not a VERY good opportunity for showing off her knowledge, as there was no one to listen to her, still it was good practice to say it over) '—yes, that's about the right distance—but then I wonder what Latitude or Longitude I've got to?' (Alice had no idea what Latitude was, or Longitude either, but thought they were nice grand words to say.)

Presently she began again. 'I wonder if I shall fall right THROUGH the earth! How funny it'll seem to come out among the people that walk with their heads downward! The Antipathies, I think—'

To add notes and highlights, simply highlight text by dragging with your mouse. This brings up options to add a note or highlight a passage in the color of your choice. It's a great way to annotate your reading material, and iBooks in El Capitan will make taking copious notes much easier than a touchscreen can. Of course, your notes, highlights, bookmarks, and last page read will be synced across all of your devices running iBooks.

You can also quiz yourself on your reading comprehension using Study Cards. Study Cards are based on items you search for or highlight, and it's a quick and easy way to study. No more index cards!

Automator

Automator is a very useful tool if you find yourself performing repetitive tasks, like renaming large numbers of files. Automator doesn't require any scripting knowledge – it's a drag and drop interface for creating actions and workflows. It includes a library of actions that you can use to build your own workflows. El Capitan includes some great updates, including nine new dictation-based workflows and improved scripting support in Photos.

Automator is worth spending some time with if you find yourself performing the same set of actions over and over again. There are numerous tutorials available online, and it doesn't take very long to get the hang of it. You can find Automator in your Applications folder or by using Launchpad.

Dashboard

The Dashboard is an area of OS X El Capitan that contains several mini-applications, or widgets. You may or may not get a lot of use out of these. You can access the dashboard by swiping to the left with three fingers, or, if you prefer, you can enable the old overlay style by visiting **System Preferences > Mission Control > Dashboard**. Change the display setting for Dashboard to Overlay if you've been missing the old widget display style in which the widgets float in over the desktop.

The default widgets are a calculator, a clock, a calendar, and a weather report. To add more or to remove widgets, click the plus or minus at the bottom left corner of the screen. Note that there are many more widgets available from Apple at http://www.apple.com/downloads/dashboard/?r=dbw.

You can drag widgets around to rearrange them. You can also organize widgets into folders if you find yourself overwhelmed with too many to fit comfortably on the screen.

Dictation

To start dictation, simply press the FN key twice. You can also start dictation from any app by using the edit menu. Click **Edit > Start Dictation**. Your computer will confirm that you're about to start using dictation. A microphone icon will appear, and when you're finished, simply click **Done** or press Enter. Dictation also supports punctuation. For example, at the end of the sentence you simply say "period." It also understands several other punctuation marks. Dictation works right out of the box and uses your Mac's built-in microphone. It isn't entirely error-free, but it still does the job pretty well. As Apple enthusiastically puts it, "talking is the new typing."

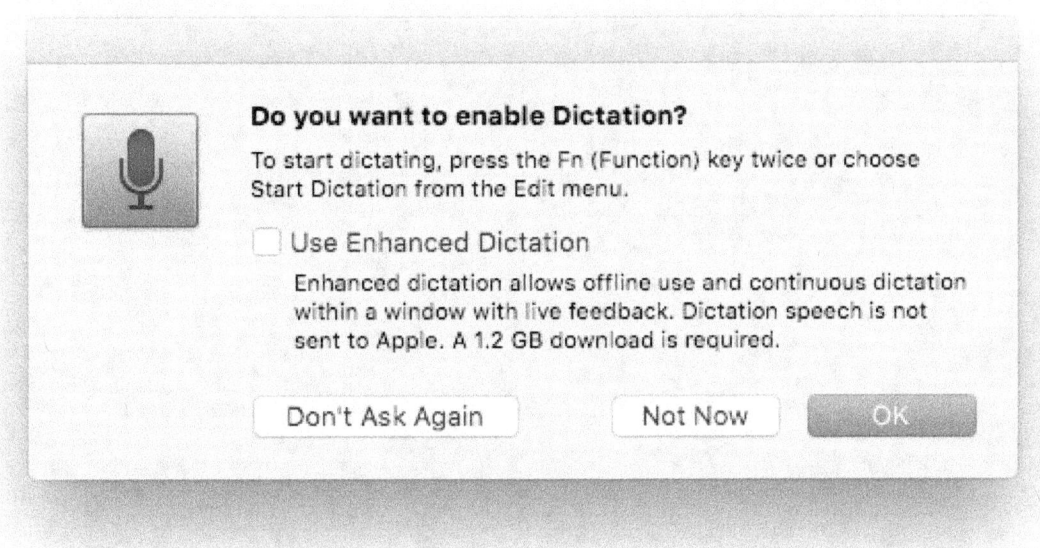

El Capitan also includes "enhanced dictation," though it's not enabled by default. Enhanced dictation happens in real time, meaning you can watch the words appear almost immediately after you say them. This makes a huge difference in Dictation's usefulness. To try it out, go to **System Preferences > Dictation and Speech**, and check "Use Enhanced Dictation."

Auto Save

OS X El Capitan continues OS X's proud tradition of excellent auto save, preserving the nerves of students and employees everywhere. El Capitan apps will automatically save your work every five minutes and provide options for reverting to previous versions. Now you can even rename files within an app by clicking the file name in the title bar and selecting **Rename** from the menu that pops up.

NOTE: The title bar renaming feature works on most Apple apps, but may not be supported by all third party software at this time.

iWork and iLife

If you are lucky enough to have a brand new Mac or MacBook, then the iWork and iLife suites ship free with your machine. iWork includes Pages, Keynote and Numbers (word processing, presentations, and spreadsheets, respectively), and iLife includes iMovie and GarageBand (note that iPhoto is no longer being developed). These are all extremely powerful programs, each deserving of their own guide. Unfortunately, those of us who downloaded El Capitan on Mac computers purchased before 2013 will still have to pay for these in the App Store. iWork apps work with Handoff.

Other Apps You'll Use Often

There are a few other apps worth knowing about inside El Capitan – you'll use them all the time, but they don't have quite as much "flash" as iTunes, iBooks, Maps, Calendar, and the like. When you need them, though, you'll be glad to know they're there waiting for you in Launchpad!

Preview is the app El Capitan uses to show you picture files and PDFs. It's a simple app, and most image files will open in it automatically. However, it includes a few useful features. You can export image files as PDF in Preview (**File > Export as PDF**) or add annotations (**Tools > Annotations**).

TextEdit is Apple's answer to Microsoft's Notepad. This is a simple plain text editor. It's certainly not fancy, but it's the kind of thing that comes in handy fairly often.

Calculator is accessible from both your Dashboard and from Launchpad. The Launchpad version isn't quite as aesthetically pleasing, but you can have it open on your desktop, making it easier to work with numbers without having to switch back and forth from your Dashboard to your desktop.

Stickies is a love it or hate it sort of app. Stickies are like post it notes for your desktop. Just open the Stickies app from Launchpad and start sticking away!

Make a note of it!

Stickies lets you keep notes (like these) on your desktop. Use a Stickies note to jot down reminders, lists, or other information. You can also use notes to store frequently used text or graphics.

• To close this note, click the close button.

• To collapse this note, double click the title bar.

Your current notes appear when you open Stickies.

3.3 Customization

It's a good idea to set up your Mac in the way that feels the most comfortable for you. This section will help you get everything set up just the way you like it.

Open up **System Preferences** (the gears icon) from the Dock. Alternatively, you can use the Apple menu in the very top left corner. This is very similar to Control Panel in Windows, and most of your customization begins here.

General Display Options (Scroll bars, Ask to Save, Recent Items)

Under **General,** you'll find some very basic options, including the option to ask to save changes before closing a document. We strongly recommend selecting this – it can save you heartache!

This is also the place where you can customize your scroll bar appearance. El Capitan hides scroll bars when they aren't in use, but if you find yourself missing them, you can bring them back under **General** in System Preferences. Select **Always** under **Show scroll bars.**

Desktop and Screen Saver

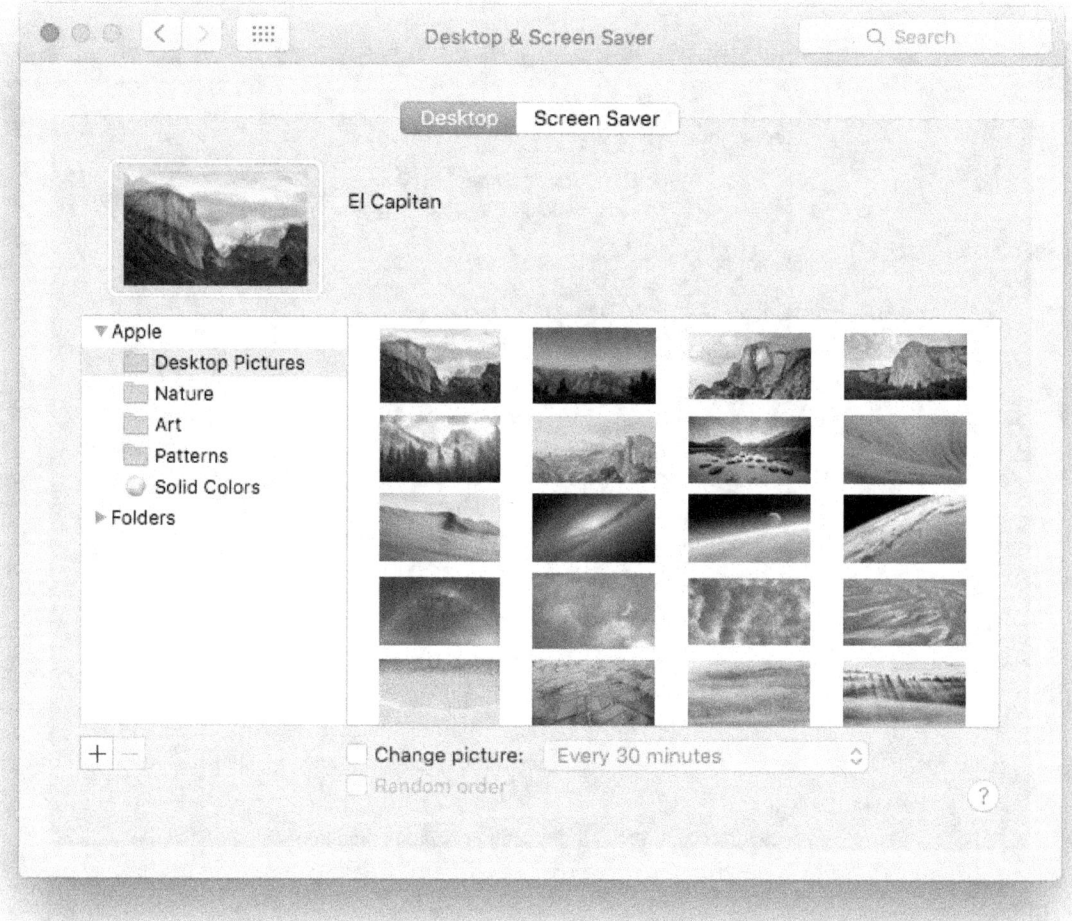

Under **Desktop and Screensaver,** you can choose your desktop background and your screensaver of choice. To choose one of your own pictures, click the **Folders** menu to expand it and then locate the image you'd like to use.

*TIP: You can also right click on any picture file in Finder or on your Desktop and choose **Set as Desktop**.*

If you'd like to use a custom screen saver, click **Screen Saver** at the top of the **Desktop and Screen Saver** System Preferences window. You can set your screen saver to one of the slideshow options and use your own photos by selecting **Choose folder** from the **Source** dropdown menu. This can be a great conversation starter at parties!

Hot Corners

To configure hot corners, visit **System Preferences > Desktop and Screen Saver > Screen Saver.** Then click **Hot Corners** on the bottom right.

Hot corners trigger actions when you move your mouse pointer over to them. You can assign a hot corner to each of the four corners on your screen, though we recommend leaving the top right corner empty or set it to Notification Center – otherwise, you'll have to be very precise when accessing your notifications area. Hot corner options include Start Screen Saver, Disable Screen Saver, Mission Control, Application Windows, Desktop, Dashboard, Notification Center, Launchpad, and Put Display to Sleep.

The best way to figure out if hot corners are a good idea for you is to try them out. You can always change or remove them if they start getting in the way!

Dock Options

You can customize the appearance of your Dock by choosing **Dock** from the System Preferences window. One popular customization is to shrink the Dock's size to **small** or to hide it altogether and then enable Magnification by checking the Magnification box. This will cause icons on the Dock to enlarge when you move the pointer over them, while saving valuable screen space when the Dock isn't in use. It's also a very aesthetically pleasing effect. Try it out!

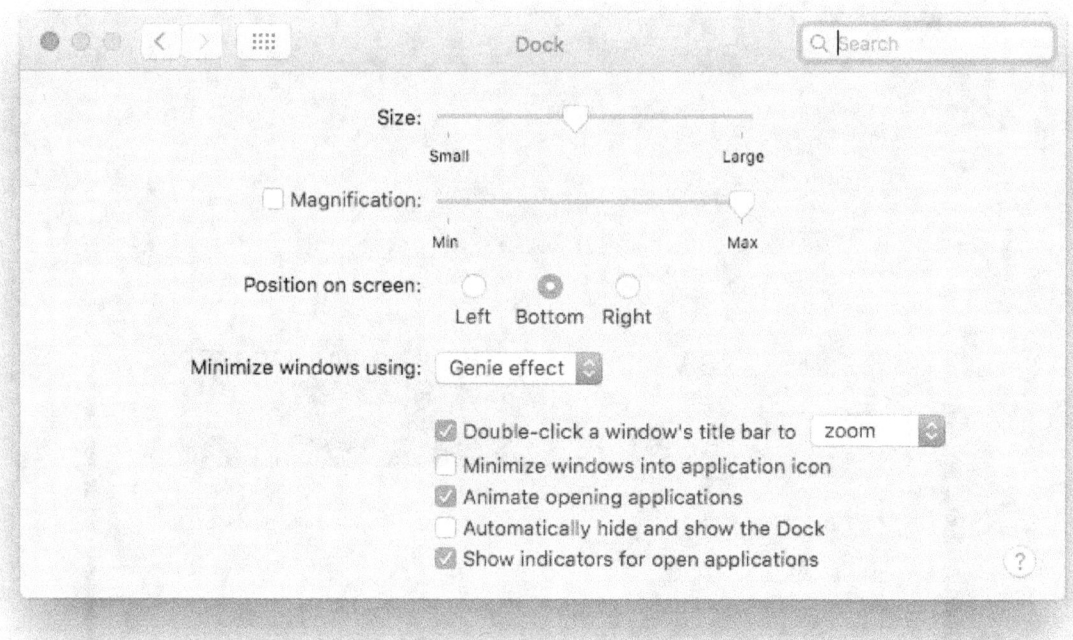

You can also change the Dock's position on the screen, hide it altogether when you're not using it, and choose animation options for opening and closing applications. Explore a little until you find the configuration that works the best for you.

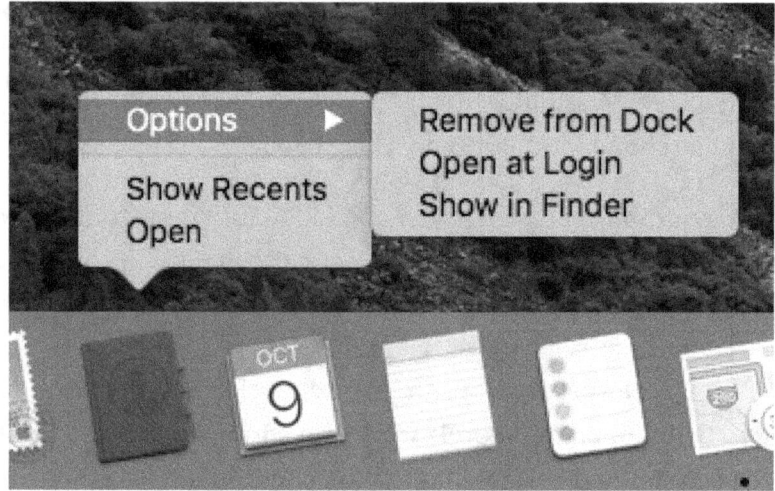

To add applications or shortcuts to your Dock, drag the application or file to the Dock and release it. To remove applications, right click on the icon in the Dock, and select **Options > Remove from Dock.** You can also instruct Mac to open an application at Login here.

Notification Center Options

You can decide what sorts of things you want popping up in your Notification Center by dragging and dropping applications from "In Notification Center" and "Not in Notification Center" in **System Preferences > Notifications** (hint: scroll down to get to the "Not in Notification Center" heading). Additionally, you can turn off Notifications sounds for individual apps, control the display of notifications, and set the number of items from each app you'd like displayed by right clicking each application.

You can also take advantage of the Do Not Disturb feature for your notifications. While you can activate this at any time by pressing the OPTION key and the + key at the same time, you can also set reoccurring Do Not Disturb periods (in case you want to get some sleep!). You can also specify contacts that you want to be able to FaceTime you, even if you are in Do Not Disturb Mode.

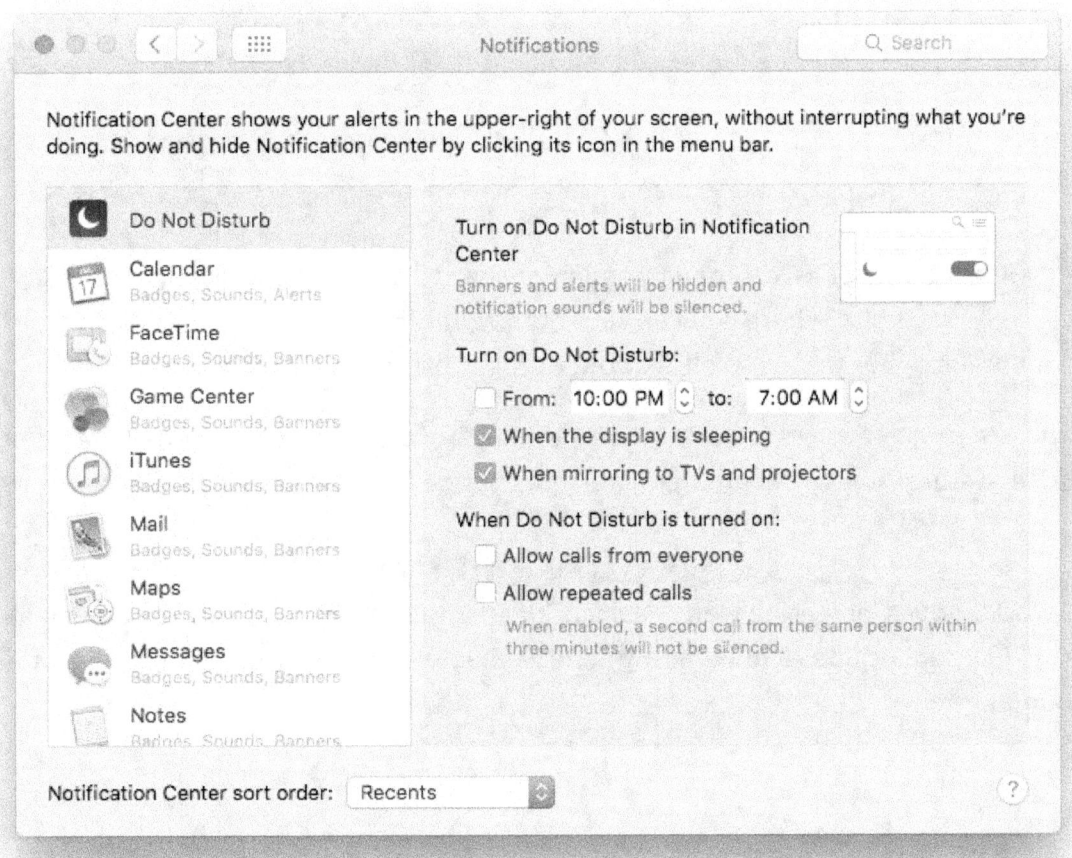

Trackpad Options

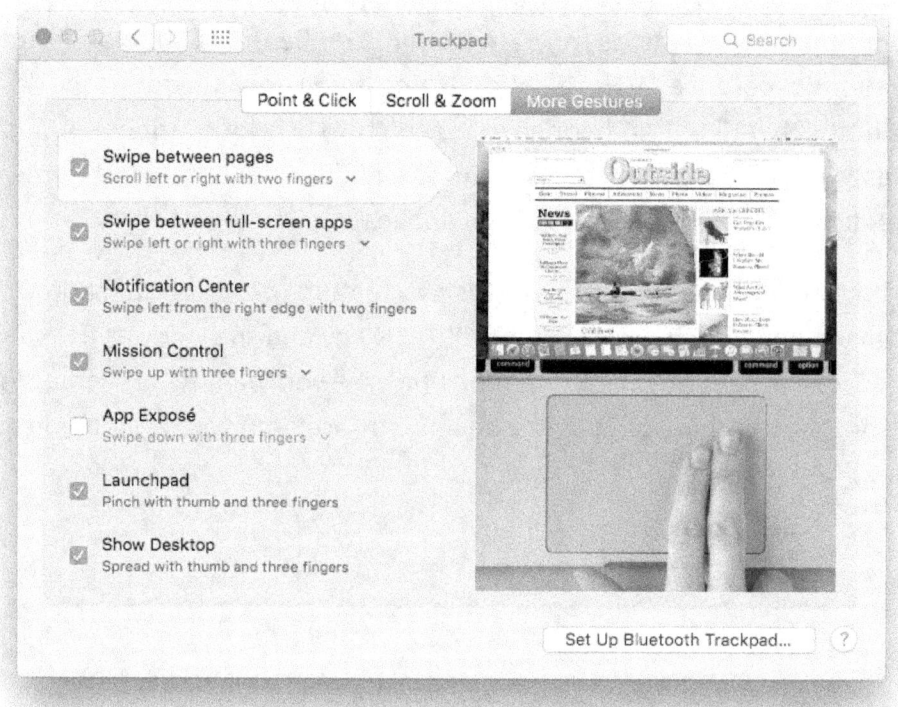

Use **System Preferences > Trackpad** to assign or change gestures according to your preferences. This is also where you can turn off natural scrolling. Deselect the "Scroll direction: natural" box under **Scroll & Zoom** to revert to "normal" scrolling.

You can also assign gestures to various tasks under **More Gestures.** Select each task you'd like to use gestures for, and then use the arrow to choose the gesture you'd like to assign.

3.4 Security and Privacy

As the world moves increasingly online, security and privacy are becoming more and more critical. El Capitan includes a number of features that will help you protect your information and your identity.

Restricting Folders from Spotlight

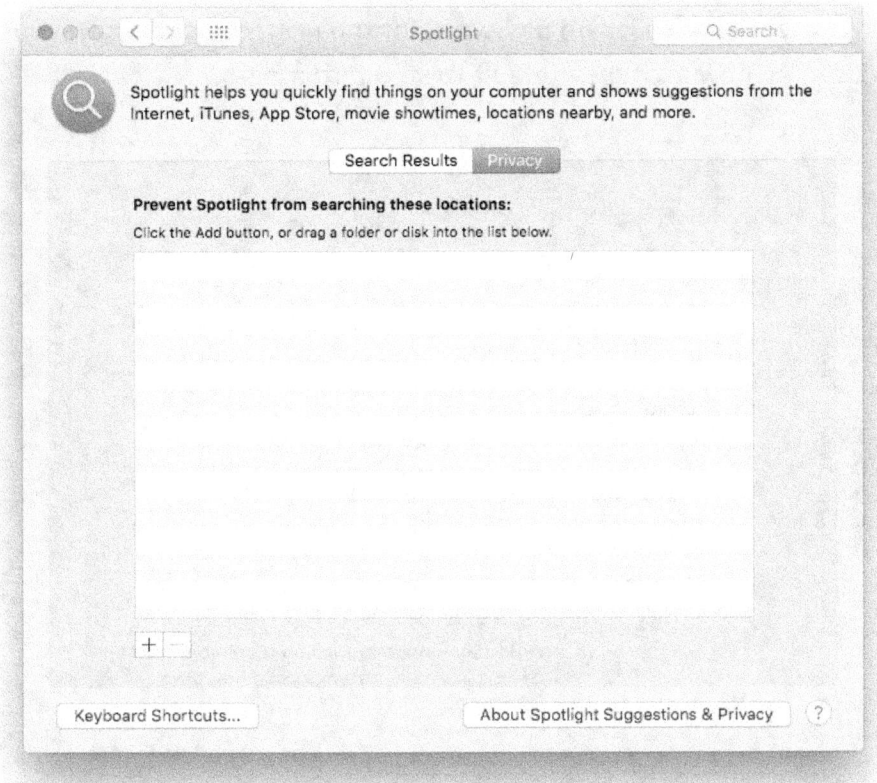

Let's say you use a family computer, and you've stored Christmas shopping lists on it. If you have folders you don't want Spotlight to search, click **Privacy** at the top of the **Spotlight** preferences window in **System Preferences**, and then use the + and – buttons at the bottom to add or remove folders from the list of folders Spotlight won't search.

User Accounts and Parental Controls

If you will be sharing your Mac with other users, including younger children, you can create multiple user accounts and manage parental controls. The primary account (the one you used when you turned on the Mac for the first time) is also the 'Account Administrator.' The account administrator has unlimited access to all areas of the computer, the ability to install and update apps, set limits for other user accounts and more.

To manage your accounts and create additional accounts, select **System Preferences -> Users & Groups.** The files, media libraries and preferences associated with each account are stored separately from other users. A user can only access his or her own information when logged in. In addition to account administrator, you can create three other account tiers: standard, managed with parental controls, and sharing. A standard account has limitless access to all applications on the Mac. With a managed account, the account administrator has placed limits on what the user can and cannot access. If you have a child and want to add parental limits, you will need to set up your child's account as a managed account.

To create a new account, click the (+) button at the bottom of the **Users and Groups** screen to create a new account. Enter a one-word user name for the account name. In El Capitan, you can use an Apple ID or a separate password for the user, depending on your preference. Select **Create User**. All new accounts default to standard access.

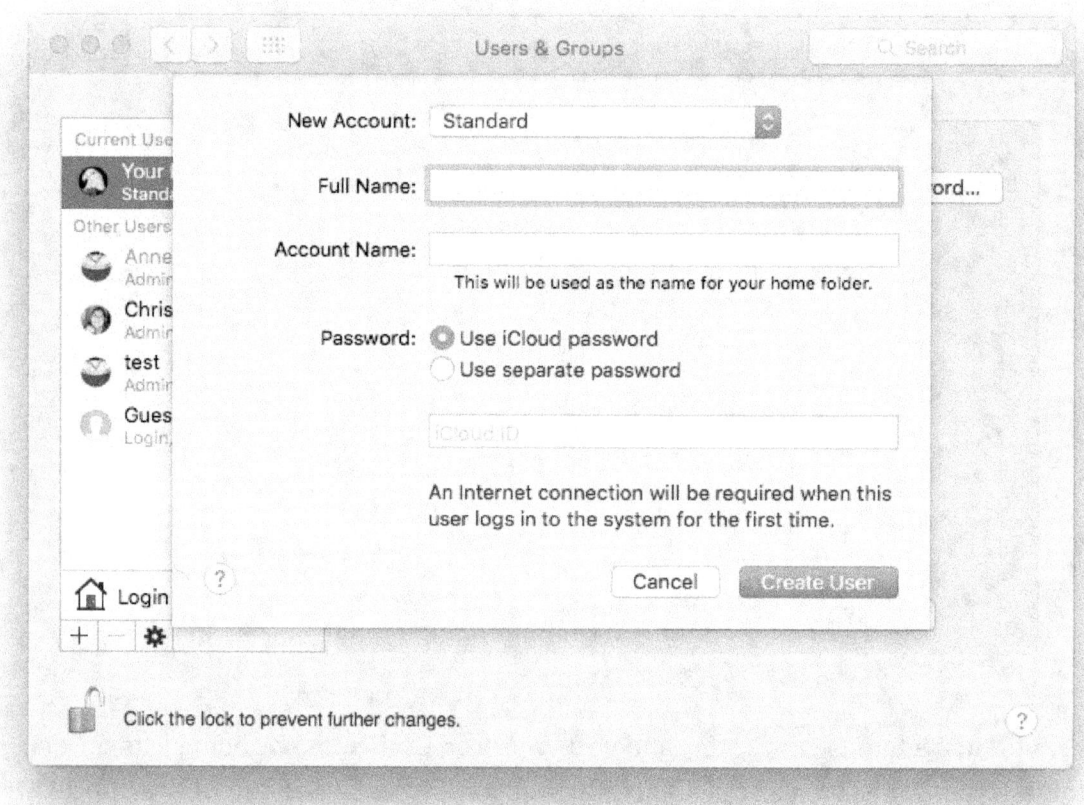

If you are a parent and want to manage your child's use of the Mac, use **System Preferences > Parental Controls.** Then customize how you'd like your child's account to access apps, the web, and other users in Game Center. You can also set time limits, and under **Other,** hide profanity from the dictionary, limit CD burning and printer access, and more.

For more information about managing a Mac with kids, check out Family Sharing in **2.6.**

Change Your Password

To set and change passwords, click the password tab in **System Preferences > Users and Groups** and select 'Change Password.' You will need to enter both your current password and a new password to successfully change it.

Private Browsing in Safari

Private Browsing allows you to browse the web without saving your history or any cookies or other site data. To turn on Private Browsing in Safari, simply open Safari and select **Safari > Private Browsing** in the main menu**.**

App Permissions

It's easy to lose track of which app integrates with what. Fortunately, El Capitan makes it easy to figure out which apps are tracking your location, which apps can access your contacts, etc. Just go to **System Preferences > Security and Privacy,** and click on the Privacy tab. Here, you'll see a list of apps on the left and the apps with permission to access them on the right.

3.5 Keyboard Shortcuts

OS X El Capitan contains numerous keyboard shortcuts that can make your life easier. There's no sense in trying to memorize the entire list, but it's a good idea to familiarize yourself with the shortcuts that can save you time. The following table is a partial list of some of the most common shortcuts. However, if there is a shortcut associated with a task, it's generally listed on the menu next to the task's name (for an example, look at the **Edit menu** in Finder to see the shortcuts for undo, redo, copy, paste and cut – these shortcuts are useful for just about anyone!).

NOTE: This list was adapted from the extensive shortcut list found on Apple's website at http://support.apple.com/kb/HT1343

Shortcut Keys	Action
⌘+A	Select All
OPTION + ⌘ + A	Deselect All
SHIFT + ⌘ + A	Open Applications Folder
⌘+C	Copy
⌘+D	Duplicate
⌘+E	Eject
⌘+I	Get Info
⌘+N	New
SHIFT + ⌘ +T	Add to Favorites
⌘+V	Paste

⌘+W	Close Window
⌘+X	Cut
⌘+1	Icon View
⌘+2	List View
⌘+3	Column View
⌘+4	Cover Flow View
⌘+TAB	Switch Application
⌘+DELETE	Move to Trash
⌘+?	Open Help
⌘+SHIFT+Q	Log Out
⌘+CONTROL+EJECT	Restart
⌘+SHIFT+3	Take screenshot
⌘+SHIFT+4	Take partial screenshot
⌘+SHIFT+4+SPACE	Take screenshot of one window
F3	Mission Control
F4	Dashboard

3.6 Accessibility

El Capitan includes a very rich accessibility feature set. Switch Control allows users who cannot operate a mouse or trackpad to use a single switch device to interact with El Capitan. The built-in screen reader VoiceOver can now analyze images for vision-impaired users. VoiceOver can also duck any other sounds your system makes and includes iBooks support. You can adjust the display to enhance the contrast, display in gray scale, or reduce transparency. You can also enable keyboard shortcuts for zooming in. Speakable Items provides a syntax for controlling your Mac with your voice instead of the keyboard. And there's more!

To explore El Capitan's accessibility options, visit **System Preferences > Accessibility.**

Part 4: Maintaining Your Mac

One of the appeals of using the Mac OS X operating system is that for the most part it maintains itself. Since it is based on the Unix operating system, Mac OS X periodically runs scripts in the background that help to keep the file system in order and the memory clear. Things like defragging the hard drive are not necessary in Mac OS X. That being said, there are a few things you can do to help keep your computer running smoothly and efficiently.

4.1 Backup Your Computer Using Time Machine

There are numerous commercial and open source backup solutions available, but one of the best solutions is built into your operating system already! Time Machine will back up all of your files, applications, and settings with minimal configuration or headache. In the case of a catastrophic event such as hard drive failure, having a Time Machine backup can allow you to quickly recover all of your data and applications, and even all of your settings (such as your desktop background and even the specific location of icons on your desktop).

You will need to buy an external USB or Thunderbolt hard drive. It is recommended to buy a drive that is larger than the current used space on your computer. For example, if you have used 100 gigabytes of space on your computer's hard drive, you should buy at least a 120-gigabyte hard drive.

Simply plug the hard drive into your computer and Time Machine will start automatically. It will ask you if you would like to use the drive as a Time Machine Backup Disk. Choose **Use as Backup Disk.**

If Time Machine does not start automatically, go to **Finder > Applications > Machine**, and click **Choose Backup Disk**. Select your new hard drive.

After you specify the drive to use as a backup, Time Machine will automatically begin backing up your data. Time Machine will perform a backup every time you plug in the drive, or, if you leave the drive plugged in, it will perform a backup each hour for 24 hours, daily backups for the past month, and weekly backups for all previous months. When the drive becomes full, it will delete the oldest backups to make more space on the drive. That way, you can rest assured that your files are being backed up without having to interact and monitor the entire backup process.

4.2 Run Software Updates

One of the best ways to keep your computer running smoothly is to run updates as they become available. These updates fix minor bugs, make your computer more secure, and sometimes add new features to Mac OS X. It is recommended that you pay special attention to running these updates when they are available. Mac OS X, by default, will prompt you when updates are available, and you need only to click **Update** and enter your password in order to run the updates. Sometimes, in the case of major updates, you will need to restart your computer to complete the update. You can click **Not Now** in the update notification if you would like to delay the updates until a more convenient time.

Third-party software (for example Microsoft Office or Mozilla Firefox) will also periodically prompt you to update; it is recommended to run these updates when they become available to keep everything running smoothly and securely.

4.3 Quitting Unused Applications

To allow frequently used programs to start quickly, Mac OS X often leaves applications running even if you have closed the window you were working on. Though it makes it faster to start these applications, if too many applications are open it can start to fill the memory and slow down the computer. To see what applications are open, simply look on the dock. Applications that are running will have a small black dot underneath them. If you see an application running that you do not expect to use for a while, it is best to quit the application by right-clicking on the application's icon and choosing "Quit". You can also quit the application by clicking the title of the application in the main menu and choosing "Quit".

Alternately, you can quit the application that is currently running by using the keyboard shortcut Command + Q.

If you've had a web browser such as Safari or Firefox running for a long time and have visited many websites and notice your computer running slowly, quitting the web browser and starting it again can help free up memory and speed things up.

If an application has crashed, you can force it to quit by clicking on the Apple icon on the top left of the screen and choosing Force Quit. Then simply choose the offending application and click Force Quit.

4.4 Restarting your computer

To restart your computer, click the Apple icon in the main menu at the top of the screen and choose "Restart."

OS X El Capitan can more or less run indefinitely without experiencing major problems. Because of this, it can be easy to forget to restart your computer periodically. Even if you're not experiencing any problems, it's never a bad idea to restart your computer every week or so. Restarting will allow the computer to "refresh" itself by automatically running scripts that tidy up your file system and refresh the memory. If you're experiencing a problem, a restart is often all it takes to get up and running again.

4.5 Keep your desktop and trash clean

OS X El Capitan creates a few special folders that give you a logical place to store files (for example, Documents, Pictures, Music, and Videos). You'll be best served by using these folders to store your data rather than just placing everything on the desktop. In addition to the "Clean Office, Clean Mind" benefits you'll receive from having a tidy desktop, this will also put less burden on the memory in your computer and improve overall performance. If you're worried about being able to find your files if they are not kept on the desktop, remember that you can always use Spotlight to very quickly find any file on your computer by clicking on the magnifying glass in the top right of the screen.

Emptying the Trash can also help free up disk space and relieve some pressure on your system's memory. To empty the trash, simply right click on the garbage can icon in your dock and choose "Empty Trash". Alternately, you can open the Trash and click the "Empty" button at the top right of the window.

4.6 Repair Permissions

In rare circumstances, it can help to repair permissions. If you have installed many pieces of software and have run many updates on your computer, sometimes the file permissions of your operating system can become a little confused, degrading overall performance.

To repair permissions on your hard drive, go to **Finder > Applications > Utilities > Disk Utility** (or simply type Disk Utility in Spotlight). From the Disk Utility pane, select Macintosh HD, and then click "Repair Permissions". This process may take a few minutes.

It's not often necessary to repair permissions on your computer, but it might be a good starting point for alleviating unexplained slowness or fixing problems with applications that previously ran just fine.

4.7 Getting Help

Unfortunately, sometimes app glitches and hardware disasters fail to respond, no matter what you try. When this happens, your best bet is to Google the problem. Googling a specific problem will turn up more answers, and do so far faster, than simply reading online Mac forums (though it's always nice to know you aren't alone in struggling with a problem). If you are one of the first to make the switch to El Capitan, you may also be able to find helpful work-around hints for app problems. If you don't find your problem, try posting all the details in a forum for assistance.

You can, of course, also check out Apple's online support. The help site includes a convenient search tool that allows you to explore the Knowledge Base, a collection of 100,000+ technical articles. Depending on whether you purchased an extended warranty with your Mac (known as Apple Care) you may be able to receive free phone or Genius bar support. If you call for help within the first 90 days of your Mac purchase, Apple Care technicians will assist you for free. You can also visit these sites for assistance:

Apple Discussion Groups - http://discussions.apple.com

Apple's help site - www.apple.com/support

4.8 Physical Maintenance

While Mac OS X is an operating system like no other, taking care of your physical Mac isn't too different from taking care of any other computer – but it's still worth mentioning! You shouldn't store your Mac in extremely cold or extremely hot temperatures. Use specially formulated screen cleaner to keep your screen bright and functioning for as long as possible. Keep your keyboard dust and gunk free, and watch out for spills. If you're not sure you're up to the task of keeping your Mac accident-free, consider purchasing an Apple Care warranty, which will protect against accidental damage.

Part 5: The Power of Free

OS X El Capitan comes with many applications that are great for doing almost everything you need to do. However, there are lots of free applications available that expand on your Mac's capabilities and can even mimic expensive software suites like Microsoft Office and Adobe Creative Suite.

Many of these programs are offered in Apple's App Store, making it easy to quickly get some of the best free apps available for Mac OS X.

Google Chrome

www.google.com/chrome

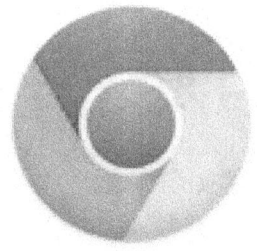

Google Chrome is an excellent alternative to Safari and has the ability to quickly synchronize information such as your bookmarks, your auto-fill information, and your browser settings wherever you use Chrome! It's been heralded for its security, speed, and ease of use compared to other available browsers. Another free browser, Firefox (www.firefox.com), is also a very popular alternative to the Safari web browser included in Mac OS X.

OpenOffice

www.openoffice.org

OpenOffice is a free and popular alternative to Microsoft's Office Suite. The full suite comes with six programs that are easy to master for anyone who's already familiar with Microsoft Office Suite. OpenOffice's applications Writer, Calc, and Impress are equivalent to the Microsoft's core applications—Word, Excel, and PowerPoint. OpenOffice also comes with programs for creating and editing vector graphics, manipulating databases, and for creating mathematical equations. OpenOffice can also save in formats that are usable by other pieces of software.

Skype

www.skype.com

Skype is a very popular app for making video calls to other Skype users, and can even be used to make calls to land line and cell phones! Using your free Skype account, you can easily connect with video and audio to any other Skype user anywhere in the world. It's a great way to get FaceTime-like connectivity with friends and family who don't own Apple devices.

Dropbox

www.dropbox.com

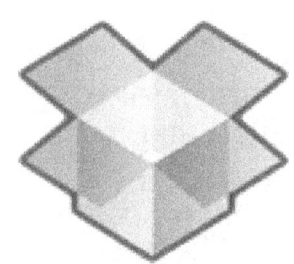

Dropbox is a powerful little program that lets you easily back up any file to the web, making that file immediately accessible to you anywhere in the world with an internet connection! You can also set up Dropbox to automatically back up a folder to the web (for example, your documents folder) to make sure you always have a copy of your important files whenever (and wherever!) you may need them. Dropbox starts with two gigabytes of storage for free, and for every friend you refer to the service, you receive an additional 500 megabytes of space! If you need more storage, you can buy additional storage space for a small fee. If you're not ready to make the switch to iCloud Drive, Dropbox is an excellent OS-agnostic alternative.

Evernote

www.evernote.com

Evernote is a great way to save anything you might be looking at on your computer. You can drag practically anything into the Evernote icon on the menu bar to have it automatically saved and cataloged at any computer you may use. Pictures, text, and even media files can be captured into Evernote for easy access later. You can even search for hand written and printed text inside of photos—great for business cards! Since it's web based, you can access these snippets anywhere with an internet connection.

Switch

www.nch.com.au/switch

Switch is the best audio converter available for OS X. The full paid version can convert pretty much any audio file format (for example, .mp3, .wav, .flac, and .wma) to any other audio format you might need. The free version will only convert to mp3, but since iTunes is quite happy with mp3 files, the free version is still a useful utility to have on hand. Great for getting those difficult audio file formats into an mp3! Switch can also be used to extract audio files from any video format (including DVDs!)

Handbrake

www.handbrake.fr

Handbrake is like Switch for video files. Unlike Switch, the full version is completely free and open source. You can easily and quickly convert between most video formats (for example, .avi, .mpg, and .wmv) to any other format you might need. The user interface might seem a little daunting to novices, but generally if you just go with the default settings you can easily get video files into any format you may need!

ClamXav

www.clamxav.com

Mac OS X is notorious for being less virus-prone than other operating systems, however the threat of malware is always present on any system. A great, free way to stay protected from malware is by using ClamXav. You can use it to directly scan a suspicious file or to scan your entire hard drive for any malicious software - Mac, Windows, or otherwise - that might be hiding out in your computer.

CCleaner

www.ccleaner.com

CCleaner is a great little app that can help get rid of unnecessary files and can quickly clear hard drive space-hogging log and tracking files. This option-rich application is the perfect tool for tidying things up, but beware: if you're not sure what a file is, it's probably better not to delete it!

VLC

www.videolan.org

The VLC media player by Videolan should be a standard for any operating system. It can play almost any type of audio or video file that you can throw at it, including DVDs and audio CDs, without having to install pesky plugins. In addition to providing support for those files that OS X can't support natively, its easy-to-use interface makes it the best choice for playing audio and video files.

Miro

www.getmiro.com

Miro is an open source application that acts like a media library for your computer. It mimics the style of iTunes (and can even use your iTunes information to get started), but can play many more types of audio and video files. It's also a quick way to find free streaming resources like Hulu, YouTube, and Vimeo all in one application. Unlike iTunes, which can just connect to the Apple iTunes Store, Miro can also connect to Amazon and Google Music to purchase and download new music and videos, making getting new media even easier!

Skitch

www.skitch.com

Skitch is by far the best, easiest to use, most feature-rich application for taking screenshots on OS X! El Capitan comes with a screen shotting utility (press command + control + shift + 3 to copy a basic screenshot to your clipboard) that works well but might be a bit unintuitive.

In Skitch, you can take screenshots of your entire screen, an open window on your desktop, or of anything that you select with your mouse. By simply dragging and dropping, you can save your screen shot in a variety of image formats. Even better, after taking your screenshot you can annotate the picture with text, arrows, and a whole variety of drawing tools. Additionally, you can easily upload the screenshot and annotations directly to the web, making it easy for you to share your image with others whom you give the link to!

Paparazzi

www.derailer.org/paparazzi

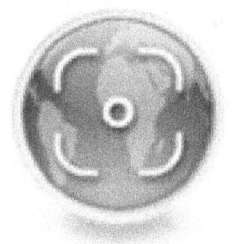

Paparazzi covers the one type of screenshot that Skitch doesn't take care of—taking a screenshot of an entire webpage, including the part "below the fold" where you would need to scroll down for it to appear on the screen. Though not often necessary, it helps to have Paparazzi installed for those times when you need to capture an entire webpage.

GIMP

www.gimp.org

GIMP, The GNU Image Manipulation Program, is a free alternative to the popular (and expensive!) Adobe Photoshop application. GIMP can do most of the things that can be done in Photoshop, and has a similar interface and workflow to Photoshop. It's a great choice for beginners looking to learn about digital photo editing and experienced editors who don't want to shell out the big bucks for Adobe's application.

Inkscape

www.inkscape.org

Inkscape is a free and easy-to-use vector graphics editor, comparable to Adobe Illustrator. It replicates many of the features and workflows available in these programs, without the headache of licensing fees. Great for the beginner graphic designer or anyone who needs to make a logo on the fly!

Google Earth

www.google.com/earth

Google Earth is a highly accurate virtual map and so much more! As a digital globe, it allows you to not only zoom in on specific places, but you can also take 3D tours of entire cities! In recent versions, you can even take 3D virtual tours of museums, monuments, and other landmarks. In recent versions, you can even explore the bottom of the ocean and the surface of Mars! Google Earth is a must-have app for OS X El Capitan.

Instapaper

www.instapaper.com

Instapaper will give you a read later bookmark, allowing you to save long websites or documents to read later when you have more time. For such a simple, free tool, it's wonderful for saving those things you'd like to come back to when you have more time. Instapaper is an excellent app for those who need to read a lot of documents on many different computers, but might not have the time.

CheatSheet

www.cheatsheetapp.com

CheatSheet is very handy Mac utility that displays a list of all the possible keyboard shortcuts that can be used within any app you're currently working in. Simply hold down the command key to get a quick list of all available keyboard shortcuts. Learning keyboard shortcuts is a powerful way to complete tasks in a fraction of the time, no matter what application you're using, and CheatSheet is the best application out there for learning these commands!

Unarchiver

unarchiver.c3.cx

OS X El Capitan has a built in archive utility that is great for unpacking .zip files, but Unarchiver will allow you to work with many more file formats (including .rar), and expand on the capabilities of OS X's built in archive utility. This app is a must have for any user who wants to compress (or uncompress) a set of files!

Text Wrangler

www.barebones.com/products/TextWrangler

OS X Capitan comes with its own text editor: TextEdit. However, TextWrangler is a much more powerful free alternative that expands on the capabilities of TextEdit. Programmers and web designers swear by this application, but it's also useful for lots of other situations - for example, being able to quickly find and replace text in a file, reading obscure or old text file formats, or quickly getting rid of the "garbage" characters that might show up from reading an unrecognized format.

Quicksilver

www.qsapp.com

Quicksilver is the most complicated to use app on this list, but it's worth the effort it takes to learn how to use it. As you use your computer, Quicksilver learns your common patterns of usage and can help to quickly replicate repeated actions that you may use over and over. It also helps to streamline tasks like sending new emails and switching between songs in iTunes. Though there's a slightly steeper learning curb, there are lots of tutorials online and the payoff is enormous!

There are tons of free apps available in Apple's App Store and elsewhere online, and it never hurts to try new things out as you come across them!

Conclusion

We hope you've enjoyed getting to know your Mac and OS X El Capitan. There's so much more to explore, though, and as you become more and more familiar with your Mac, you'll discover new and exciting ways to use it that we've never even thought of. Those possibilities are just part of the fun of owning a Mac. As you develop new habits and new user needs, you'll find ways to adapt your machine to your unique personality and requirements. Mac's flexibility and ease of use will make this a fun and easy process, freeing up your mental energy for working and playing on your Mac.

At this point, you should have a good foundation for finding thousands of answers to the question, "What can Mac do for you?" - enjoy the journey!